ENGLISH LANGUAGE TEACHING IN INDIA
(Problems and Issues)

QAISER ZOHA ALAM

PUBLISHERS & DISTRIBUTORS (P) LTD

7/22, Ansari Road, Darya Ganj, New Delhi
Tel.: +91-11-4077 5252, 2327 3880
E-mail: orders@atlanticbooks.com
Web: www.atlanticbooks.com

Published by Atlantic Publishers & Distributors (P) Ltd., 2024
Reprint 2016, 2018, 2024

Printed & bound in India by Atlantic Print Services

To
My Mother

PREFACE

The book introduces some of the major areas that students and teachers of English should understand in order to follow a scientific approach. It contains essays many of which have already appeared elsewhere. The essays have been carefully revised and modified before inclusion in this book. It is hoped that my readers will find the book useful, interesting and stimulating. The conclusions made in the essays and the pedagogical implications should be of much help to them. I shall consider myself amply repaid if this book promotes further discussion, raises some critical questioning and encourages experimentations and innovations. Needless to say, the book covers many topics that find place in the syllabi of our universities. I wish to offer my thanks to all the writers whose writings have been of help to me (whether acknowledged in the book or not). My thanks are also due to Dr. K.R. Gupta, Managing Director, M/s Atlantic Publishers and Distributors, for his friendly cooperation and for having much patience. However, I have only myself to blame for the inadequacies present in the book.

QAISER ZOHA ALAM

CONTENTS

1

THE TEACHING OF ENGLISH IN INDIA : CHANGING SCENARIO

Although the history of the English language in India can be traced back to the 31st of December, 1600, the day on which Queen Elizabeth I of England granted a charter to the "Governor and Company of Merchants of London trading with the East India". English education was in fact introduced in India in the middle of the nineteenth century. If we confine our discussion to universities alone, three universities were established, one each at Calcutta, Bombay and Madras, in 1857. The Senate of the University of Calcutta adopted a resolution in 1861 that all examinations should be conducted in English. Needless to say, this compelled all schools to introduce English as a subject at a very early stage. Thus over a hundred years ago *i.e.* when the British introduced the modern system of English education in India, the study of English was an important part of the liberal and humanistic discipline. Sir Henry Maine, the Vice-Chancellor of the University of Calcutta in the 1860's, noticed the ambition of all its graduates to write the finest English possible. Sir Henry was one of the rare Englishmen of old days who recognised that the English of some of us was very good, and he raised his voice against the chorus of jeers at Babu English from the majority of his countrymen in India. The teaching of English in the Indian Universities, however, followed a set pattern. For all we know, the then University of London provided the model. However, the traditional approach to the teaching of English came in for severe criticism later.

The focus of our ELT programmes and the role of English in our educational system have been shifting over the years. In 1917, the Calcutta University Commission took note of the rapid decline in academic standards in all subjects specially English and stressed the importance of the study of English as part of general education in India. The commission considered English indispensable to the higher education in India at that time. According to the commission some of the causes of the deterioration in the quality of the teaching of English were lack of contact with teachers who spoke English as their mother tongue, unsuitability of the lecture method and a lack of systematic instruction in spoken English.

The commission recommended a progressive reduction in the use of English as a medium of instruction upto the Matriculation stage and its retention as the medium above that stage, the adoption of scientific methods of teaching English, the introduction of more highly trained teachers and more difficult tests (for all) of a practical knowledge of English. Interestingly, the commission found that the student displayed a disquieting preference for literary studies. During the 30s the regional languages were made the medium of instruction which resulted in an alarming deterioration in the standards of the teaching and learning of English.

The teaching of English in our colleges and universities received a major set-back after independence because of the prevailing psychological attitude. The regionalisation of the medium of instruction at the university level resulted in an inadequate exposure to the English language. The examination system in use was largely unrealistic and the text books rather outdated. All this led to a sharp decline; the people concerned have taken note of the growing inadequacy of the teaching of English in colleges.

Once again, a number of commissions and study groups stressed the need for the rationalization of the English curricula, text books and examinations. The 'service' nature of the teaching of English has been largely realized and also the need of the diversification of courses to suit the divergent requirements of different categories of students of science, commerce and humanities and consequently of the suitable changes in teaching techniques. In fact, the teaching of English now aims at developing (in the students) the communication skills.

The Radhakrishnan Commission (1948) recommended the continuance of the study of English. "English should be studied in high schools and in the universities in order that we might keep ourselves in touch with the living stream of evergrowing knowledge."

The Kunzru Committee (1955) recommended that the teaching of English literature should be related to the study of Indian literatures so that apart from its value for linguistic purposes, it could be an effective means of stimulating critical thinking and writing in the Indian languages. The committee stressed the importance of the use of special methods in English language teaching and the study of linguistics as the essential prerequisites for ensuring adequate proficiency in English at the university stage. Pattison (1962) takes note of the fact that though the All India Seminar on the Teaching of English in secondary schools held at Nagpur in 1957 set up the objective that within a period of six years of the high school course the pupils should be enabled to attain a working knowledge of English, the university entrance and intermediate examinations demand the odd assortment of literary texts ranging from Shakespeare to Lamb's essays and taking in Keats and Shelley and a few other major poets on the way. Pattison is at a loss to find how one progresses from a working knowledge of English (*i.e.* 2,500 essential words) to these pieces of literature.

According to the recommendation of the official Language Commission (1956), English should be taught as "a language of comprehension rather than as a literary language so as to develop in the students learning it a faculty of comprehending writings in the English language, more specially those relating to the subject matter of their specialised fields of study". Randolph Quirk (in his Report on English Teaching in India, 1963) also found the standards of English teaching deplorable and stressed the need for reform and experiment. Kothari Commission (1964) emphasized the role of English as a library language.

The report of the Study Group I (1965) also makes a special mention of the deteriorating standards of English. The report says that scripts are, interestingly enough, assigned marks by university examiners not for what the examinees have said but what they meant to say. The group has recommended a programme for teaching English and, importantly, comprehension receives more attention in this programme than expression. The Group notes that better comprehension of written materials in English is a skill as essential as ever at the postgraduate level. That is why, the Group recommends that English should be taught for all the three years and suggests that there should be one paper on language skill, another on skills through prescribed texts and a half paper in summary and translation. Two optional sections have been recommended in the M.A. course. The first one is language oriented and the second literature oriented. The Group recommends *viva voce* test as a part of the M.A. examination to test the candidate's spoken English. Unluckily not many universities adopted this pattern rigorously. It is significant that the Group has drawn a distinction between a lecturer in the English language and a lecturer in English literature and wants the students to have the choice to specialize either in literature or in language and has also suggested that universities should have two different departments. The Group has emphasized the importance of first rate research on the teaching of English in India and has also taken note of the fact that the younger lecturers are almost as incorrect in their use of English as the pupils themselves. I am reminded here of a talk given by R E. Underwood, the British Council expert, at the Nagpur session of the All India English Teachers' Conference. Underwood discussed university education in India and identified three main problem areas. They are interconnected and concern

(a) the college students,

(b) the college text,

(c) the college lecturer.

Thereafter, Underwood went on to describe each one of them at length.

The average college student

1. (a) cannot write acceptable English,
   (b) cannot understand spoken or written English,
   (c) is very slow at reading;
2. (a) poses a problem to the lecturer,
   (b) causes various solutions to be proposed by the universities to deal with them;
3. (a) is aware of national controversy over the role of English in India,
   (b) wonders how seriously he needs to take the subject.

The average college text

(1) is treated as though it was God-given;

(2) tries to meet the needs of two quite different sets of students—

(a) the good ex-English medium (ex-vernacular medium),

(b) the average-to-poor (ex-English medium) ex-vernacular medium;

(3) contains passages not primarily selected for purposes of language learning and development of reading skills;

(4) contains no glossary and no text-based remedial language exercises.

The average college lecturer

(1) has studied hard for his M.A. in *literature* and is largely unwilling and unprepared to teach *language*;

(2) prefers the lecture to the dialogue;

(3) is disinclined to risk exposure by preparing his own language-teaching materials;

(4) may not speak and write correct English him/herself.

"In hundreds of classrooms in India to-day, Shakespeare, the first poet in the world ... is perishing ... for... not being understood"—says Nagarajan who has gathered a number of interesting excerpts from the annotated editions of the plays of Shakespeare published for Indian students, Nagarajan has also looked at another kind of evidence about Shakespeare in Indian universities—the question papers. He thinks that the question papers reflect the emphases of teaching, the approaches to the text favoured at the time. For this purpose he has looked through the question papers for the B.A., the Honours and when the course was instituted, the M.A., set from 1865 to about 1890 in the universities of Madras, Bombay and Calcutta, occasionally Punjab and Allahabad also. The major types of questions that used to be set in the years 1865 to 1890 are the following: questions regarding the reproduction from a memory of a passage, the first line being given, citation of parallels; philological notes on words and phrases; questions on authorship and chronology; down-to-earth questions calling for information about the facts of the story and occasionally theme questions and the questions on the moral of the play. The drawing of morals seems to have been a characteristic of Shakespearean teaching in those days. Those earlier teachers seem to have demanded a much closer knowledge of the text than we do. Their concern for Shakespeare's language was unfortunately too often narrowly philological.

It should be remembered that the Report of the Makerere Conference on the Teaching of English as a Second Language clearly recognized that study of literary works played a vital role in 'language learning' and that literary studies were useful because they offered the learner other advantages besides greater linguistic proficiency. Holloway (1962) has noted that the present very rapid expansion of language studies ensures that the study of literature will be seen as a useful adjunct to language study. Among the advantages offered by literary studies, as Holloway has noted, are judgement (both intellectual and moral), cogency and flexibility of mind, maturity of understanding, and a sense of evidence, of detail, and of history and, at the same time, proficiency in English makes a major culture available to the learners through literature. Even Gokak (1962) considers it essential that the teaching of English literature to those who are equipped for it should be developed into a helpful and life-giving discipline though he admits that the approach of the non-British student to English literature is in many ways bound to be different from that of a British student. Both Gokak and Holloway have spoken on the modernizing influence that a study of English literature has exercised overseas. Pattison (1962) also asserts that literature is useful even in language learning: "There is always a need for everyday language, and narrative and drama give contexts in which that language can be shown in operation—a vital part of language learning." The imported courses, Pattison thinks, "aim at producing literary critics and scholars .... But what is the function of critics in the country that has few readers". He remarks that unless English literature can be made functional in a situation, there is little hope of making it genuinely educational. I.A. Richards (1962) does not approve of separating language from literature—he does not like "thinking only or chiefly about English literature in any sort of separation from a steady advance—with standards lively and alert from the start—into the effective, the efficient, use of general, necessary English". A typical pedagogical justification that has historically been given for the value of literature to the pupil makes reference to "various aspects of character-building and intellectual, moral and personal development". Jo McDonough (1977) asserts that the study of literature is still dominant in many language situations and argues that the role and status of literary study should depend on a careful analysis of learners needs. In conclusion, we can plead that this should be realized now that the focus of English teaching has to be on the teaching of language rather than on literature. The literature is, in the process, being given its true place as vehicle of communication and, in the context of language instruction pedagogy, the literary texts are being employed keeping the 'language scheme in the foreground' (Mohan, 1975). The language through literature series prepared at the Central Institute of English and Foreign Languages, Hyderabad, is an obvious example. The traditional literary approach is being found to be out-dated and ineffective (Study Group : 1971; CIEFL 1977). As the state of affairs exists at the moment, one university after another has not only changed to an Indian language as the medium of instruction but also made the teaching of English as a language optional. Parasher's (1979) results show that a majority of his subjects think English to be the most suited medium of education beyond the primary level (Postgraduate 94.8%, professional/technical training 95.7%). Paresher finds that English is dominant in the domains of friendship, education, government and employment. According to Jain (1974), several imperatives have, since independence, dictated why English should be taught and learnt in India—the status imperative, the political imperative, the commercial imperative, the cultural imperative and the academic imperative. He concludes that "we should learn English for academic purposes. It amounts to learning English at a very competent level. And there is no short cut to it". Interestingly, Jain (1974), talks of "the shifting official policy from no English, to optional English, to limited English".

Talking of the courses, those in use before 1950 have been labelled traditional. The medium of instruction then was English and the syllabuses were literature oriented. The courses in use between 1950 and 1975 were, by and large, structural or formal. Now English was a second language and there was an apparent inclination towards language in these courses as against literature as in traditional ones. English was studied now for general purposes and the methodology adopted was oral, situational and grammatical. The usage was now taught indirectly through experience and practice. It is difficult to label the courses in use after 1975 because there are very many categories of them but for want of a better term they are named 'new' type courses. These are generally functional, communicational or notional and have been prepared bearing in mind the fact that English is now chiefly a 'service' subject and a library language. There is a greater concern now for the learner's needs: it is a case of shift of emphasis from the subject to the learner. It may be noted here that the above is a very broad and rough classification and the labels have been given only for convenience.

REFERENCES

CIEFL, 1977 : Syllabus Reform in English — *UGC* National Workshop.

Jain, M.P., 1974 : Academic Imperatives of Learning English in India. Book Talk. Vol. V, No. 2.

McDonough, Jo, 1977 : English Language Teaching and the role of literature. *IJOAL*, Vol. III, No. 2.

Mohan, Ramesh, 1975 : 'Preface' *to Language through literature* (II), *CIEFL.*

Nagarajan, S., 1978 : The Teaching of Shakespeare in India. In : Mohan, Ramesh (ed.) *Indian Writing in English*, Madras : Orient Longman.

Parasher, S.V., 1979. Educated Indian Bilinuals' attitudes to English. *IJOAL* (Indian Journal of Applied Linguistics), Vol. V, No. 2.

Press, John (Ed.), 1963 : *The Teaching of English Literature Overseas*, London: Methuen.

Quirk, Randolph, 1963 : 'A Report on English Teaching in India', University College of London.

Study Groups I & II, 1965 and 1971. Reports on Teaching of English.

2

Literary Criticism Can Wait

As the Education Commission had pointed out about two decades ago, the teaching of English as a skill and as literature should be clearly differentiated. The scales have often been heavily tilted in favour of literature. This needs to be corrected. The poetry selections are still dominated by Shakespeare, Blake, Wordsworth, Tennyson, De la Mare, Davies, Eliot and others. Shakespeare's plays are even now prescribed in some form or the other. A researcher has noted that even in the short Shakespeare edition of Julius Caesar, there are 154 archaic words and 400 sentences containing old-fashioned elements of structure and vocabulary. One wonders how the book gets prescribed for students who do not even know the rudiments of modern English usage, who are yet to be taught how to make the subject and the verb agree. Examination procedures are often so clumsy and antiquated that a student can pass by memorizing summaries of passages dictated by his teacher without reading the texts prescribed or trying to learn a word of English. The course often degenerates into a blind alley and encourages a memorizing and point-grabbing mind and not a thinking mind. The UGC Study Group had also highlighted the need to replace the existing English courses by a course in language skills. The Group had recommended that at the degree level teaching should equip students with communication skills necessary to cope with the predictable situations they were likely to encounter.

The focus of English teaching at the undergraduate level now, therefore, should be on the teaching of language rather than on literature. "The shift in emphasis from literature to language is a happy shift indeed, and a sensible shift too. It is not elegance and grace and style we crave for today, it is rather a working knowledge of the language, achievement of an acceptable standard, both in comprehension and expression" (Mathur, 1982). It is, however, uncharitable to analogise the learning of English in India today with the learning of Latin in the medieval era, when the study of literature became vestigial in the curriculum and, allegedly, a narrow careerism became a motivation. Although this task can be performed by a communication course as well, the literary texts are now being increasingly employed in the context of language teaching keeping the 'language scheme in the foreground'. "Language through literature" course prepared at the Central Institute of English and Foreign Languages, Hyderabad, exposes the students to the living language, as it exists today. The approach of the course designers is not historical or rhetorical; they do not wish to introduce the students to literary landmarks. Both language controls and cultural controls have been exercised. Several courses designed after 1975 are generally functional, communicational or notional and have been prepared bearing in mind the fact that English is now chiefly a 'service' subject and a library language. There is now a greater concern for the learner's need.

Use of Media and Technology

English by Radio and TV courses now in use have not been necessarily based on textbooks. In fact, they attempt to teach English through dramatized stories, anecdotes, conversations and the like. The basic objective of these media courses is to expose the learners to acceptable models of English being used in different situations. The programmes have been popular and could be considered potentially effective. Language laboratories have been found useful for teaching a language but even now there are very few laboratories in the country. A language laboratory is not meant to teach merely the phonetics and the repetitive drills : it can be effectively used for listening comprehension, reading, testing and evaluation (Pattanayak, 1971). Wiring three rooms as an extension of the laboratory and broadcasting lessons to students sitting in all three rooms simultaneously was an experiment initiated at the Wilson College, Bombay, with a view to solving the problem of large classes. It was an experiment worth pursuing. TV sets were provided to government schools in Delhi and other cities and they beam special programmes but most TV sets do not work (Rai, 1983). The Paul Neurath Report has confirmed the efficacy of the school TV. Even in an ESP situation, Video, an increasingly affordable teaching aid, has been found useful in developing study skills (Kennedy, 1979). If the instructor uses some ingenuity and takes care to prepare lessons carefully, the VCR can be the focal point of a successful and well-rounded EFL class (Hall, 1986). There is a feeling, however, that the programmed materials or those used for mass media may sometimes reduce the teacher to secondary importance or the teacher becomes just a 'manager' or 'facilitator' of learning.

The computer also opens up possibilities for language teaching though computer-assisted ELT is still in its infancy. The vast potential still remains largely untapped. To cite an example, the programming in the computer presents a series of interconnected problems to the student. As the student answers each question or solves each problem in the series, the answers are compared against a standard list for acceptability. If the student is correct, he automatically moves to the next problem and, consequently, gradually increases his knowledge of some specific central issue. If he commits an error, the programme directs him to re-do the same ground or to an auxiliary remedial series of problems. It is interesting to note that the student is rewarded immediately, or corrected and allowed to continue at his pace.

Bombay University Syllabus

The University of Bombay has dropped English as a compulsory paper for all three years of science and commerce students and it has been ordained that even arts students would be required to take a paper in English only in their first year. Needless to say, the university has considerably devalued the learning of the English language. The university has had the good sense at least to introduce a communication skills paper for the first year B.A. (the only compulsory English paper in any faculty). It has jettisoned Hardy and Galsworthy in favour of such elementary but useful skills as comprehension, letter writing, answering a phone or disagreeing with someone courteously. However, if these courses have to be effective, large classes should be replaced by tutorial batches. Although in operation for much too short a period only, this syllabus has been, by and large, a change of far-reaching consequences. The framers of the syllabus have recommended a number of books and the teacher has the freedom to select any one to be taught in the class. Certainly, this appears to be a step in the right direction—

books have been used as a means and not as the end. Significantly, the question papers in the examinations do not carry any questions from these books as the proficiency in the language is tested and not the capacity to paraphrase or memorize. The students are expected to attempt the tasks assigned by making use of the language in real life situations. It may also be mentioned here that questions are set in such a way that even those with average proficiency in the language can secure pass marks. Undoubtedly, this kind of syllabus is likely to check the tendency to learn language skills by memorizing answers from the Bazar notes. The fact remains, however, that the time is not ripe yet to pass judgement as to how the approach has been working. We have to watch closely the way the syllabus is executed and the results it achieves.

The Bangalore Project

The Bangalore Project, also known as Communicational Teaching Project, has been tried in schools in Bangalore and Madras and has aroused considerable interest and controversy. The Regional Institute of English, Bangalore, resorted to the project after the experts there realized the ineffectiveness of the structural approach as a means of English teaching. It was felt that the approach had failed to encourage learners to use what they supposedly knew. The project is still at an experimental stage though the results achieved at Madras, Bangalore and Cuddalore have been encouraging. When expedited fully, the project is expected to serve as an empirical test of the hypothesis that English can be learnt without explicit teaching, through concentration on language-using tasks (Brumfit, 1981). The project is actually a detailed and arduous application and trial of the approach to communicational teaching and based on the distinction made by Widdowson (1978) between 'usage' and 'use'. Hymes (1972) has aptly remarked that the rules of grammar will be useless without the rules of use. G.B. Shaw wrote to *The Times* in 1907 about the split infinitives: "It is of no consequence whether he decided to go quickly, quickly to go or quickly go. The important thing is that he should quickly go." Churchill commented against sentences that went to considerable lengths to avoid a prepositional ending: "This is the sort of English up with which I will not put." Widdowson wants language teaching to move away from an emphasis on sentences in isolation to the use of sentences in combinations. In recent years language teaching has, more or less, come to mean teaching people to communicate. One wonders why students should spend more time *talking about* language than *using* language to communicate.

As English is a highly idiomatic language, literal translations usually sound odd. Roussel (1983) suggests *Speak English*—a book which offers a graded selection of idiomatic conversations corresponding to a variety of everyday life situations. The stories in the English comics are likely to keep up a reader's interest while exposing him to the 'real thing'. It may be particularly useful, as Roussel suggests, if from a very early stage one writes down phrases rather than words, and in context rather than isolated. This enables the learner to get used to functioning in a target language instead of resorting to translations. Roussel rightly finds W.S. Allen's *Living English Structure* (Longman) a good book as it combines an explicit presentation and structural drills. There are a number of games also which are not only enjoyable but useful from this point of view.

The Bangalore Project appears to be a good one and may succeed particularly where the objective is to teach English as a tool of communication. The communicational approach is a situation-based teaching. The learners react to communicational situations and, consequently, learn the language. Prabhu (1980) emphatically remarks: "What we are saying is not 'English for communication' but 'English through communication'." Prabhu's (1982) Procedural syllabus consists of tasks which are carefully graded, functionally grouped and systematically recycled and are supposed to activate and extend the 'analytic competence' of the learner.

The Bangalore Project makes a serious attempt to provoke the learners out of their traditional passivity and challenges them to use English for effective communication. The teaching in this project does not depend on a textbook: it rather depends on a teacher's ability to develop an atmosphere where the learners really use the language. In a 'communicational' classroom, the focus is not on a syllabus but on a list of notions or concepts to be introduced as well as the different functions of the language to be learnt. It emphasizes the pupil's acquisition of communicative competence, acquired through constant exposure, than linguistic competence, acquired through conscious learning (*what* rather than *how*). It goes without saying that a learner performs certain general functions like requesting, greeting, warning, interrogating, apologizing, inviting, expressing gratitude, expressing regret, complaining, conveying a message and exchanging facts etc. That is why, he actually needs language forms like structures, phrases and words to translate his thoughts into concrete forms and to put forward propositions with appropriate linguistic etiquette. Davies and Widdowson (1974) have stressed the value of written language—"There is a strong case for the teaching of communicative competence through written language, since, generally speaking, in second language teaching it is only through the written mode that the way language actually functions as communication can be satisfactorily demonstrated." The communicative approach requires the integration of linguistic skills and communicative abilities. At least four modes of communication are well-recognised—gestures, speech, writing and graphics. Communication among human beings in any social situation resorts to all the four modes in different proportions. Johnson (1982) has set out five principles which teachers should bear in mind when designing a communicative syllabus:

(i) Information transfer
(ii) Information gap
(iii) Task dependency
(iv) Correction for content
(v) Jigsaw.

Since most of the activities require the use of more than one skill at a time, the various combinations of skills so often present in authentic communication should also be taken into account. It should be noted, however, that the communicative language teaching does not give rise to much enthusiasm any longer and has become a field of controversies in India.

What people want to do with language, as Wilkins (1976) points out is more important than mastery of the language as an unapplied system. Wilkins has advanced his theory of notional syllabus. He recommends notional syllabus because, as he observes, it takes the communicational facts of language into account from the beginning without losing sight of the grammatical and situational factors. The experiments carried out at Loyala College, Madras, produced an experimental paradigm which could serve as a framework for second language teaching-learning. The Loyala experiment tried to shift the focus to tasks promoting the actual involvement and engagement of the learners in the process of learning and performing in the language — the experience of learning through involvement of the student and the teacher (Xavier, 1988)

ESP (English For Specific Purposes)

In recent years such acronyms as EGP (English for General Purposes), ESP (English for Specific Purposes), EIP (English for Instrumental Purposes), EST (English for Science and Technology), EAP (English for Academic Purposes) and EOP (English for Official Purposes) etc. have gained considerable currency. Robinson (1980) defines ESP in terms of what might broadly be seen as language-situations and functions in various combinations. The attempt is to teach a certain group of people *e.g.*, the scientists, just what they need to the exclusion of everything else. As a result, the concept of deciding the specific needs and teaching only that much was developed. It may be profitable to begin with Error Analysis with a view to specifying the students' needs. The UGC Study Group had also emphasized that one general course of English for everybody would hardly serve the purpose and that specific courses for specific needs should be offered. The report of the Education Commission (1964-66) claims that where such courses have been tried, they have proved helpful in enabling the students to use English as a library language in their own fields far more efficiently than a General English course would be. Of late, intense interest has been taken in ESP and new courses and materials in this area have been produced.

Interestingly, some see ESP as the 'communicative approach' carried to its logical conclusion whereas others see it as the field of study that led the way in the development of 'communicative approach.' Its specificity has been apparently rigorously founded on two areas of study—*i.e.*, needs analysis and register analysis. Sinclair (1978—Quoted by Roberts, 1982) feels that a new flexible approach based on online (concurrent) needs analysis acquires more importance than offline (pre-course) needs analysis. Register analysis, too, has not come up to expectations. The development of computer programmes may make lexical counts in any area possible. Widdowson (1977) asserts that "in ESP a communicative approach seems to be the obvious one to adopt because even the most elementary assessment of needs reveals that learners will have to put the language they learn to actual use outside the language teaching context". The communicative approach to ESP has been attempted by some select specialists in their organizations. Many want ESP to be socialized to meet the speakers' 'social communicative needs'. The recent approach to ESP tries to characterize the language of that particular branch in terms of specific speech acts relevant to that discourse rather than the lexical items and syntactic patterns.

It should be borne in mind, however, that many teachers just cannot imagine teaching a language without a textbook. They may feel a little awkward and out of place if the book is taken away from them. Also, we are definitely in a fool's paradise if we think that all teachers, irrespective of their equipment, can keep creating 'communication' situations for a number of days. It should be remembered, therefore, that for the success of English through communication or English without textbook approach, resourceful and imaginative teachers with command over the language, are required. We find it advisable, at any rate, to think of reorganizing our teaching programmes in such a way that the oral and written communicational aspects of English get more prominence. Language is, in fact, best learnt when it is taught as a means of communication. It should be realized that the study of English is primarily the study of the process of how to communicate something to somebody with the maximum of clarity and effect that is best suited to a particular situation. It is human psychology to take interest in things socially desirable and immediately useful.

In R.K. Narayan's *The English Teacher*, Rangappa, the Lecturer in Philosophy tells the protagonist. Krishna, the English Teacher at Albert Mission College, Malgudi that "English department existed solely for dotting the i's and crossing the t's". While taking stock of his daily life. Krishna observes that he got up at eight every day, "read for the fiftieth time Milton, Carlyle and Shakespeare, looked through compositions". As a matter of fact, how much attention and time should be devoted to language and how much to literature and how to mix the two in a palatable dose, have been issues that the teacher of English in India has been facing perennially. However, at least two marked tendencies in English language teaching at the undergraduate level in India at the moment come to the forefront — (a) that literature has been gradually losing the pride of place it had in the courses and (b) that there has been a clearly perceptible emphasis on the language skills and communicative competence. The learner needs to internalize the skill with a view to using the same in day-to-day affairs of both his chosen profession and life : literary criticism can wait.

REFERENCES

Apte, M. 1980. Developing Communicative Competence In *ESL. CIEFL* Newsletter, Vol. VI, Nos. 3 and 4.

Bhargava, R., 1986. Communicative language Teaching : A Case of Much Ado about Nothing, RUSIE-18. Jaipur.

Brumfit, C. 1981. Notices (Note on the Bangalore Project), *BAAL* Newsletter, 12.

Das, M. 1980. *ESP* and its Relevance to the Teaching of English in India, *Journal of ELT* (India), Vol. XV, No. 1.

Davies, A. and Widdowson, H.G. 1974. *Reading and Writing Edinburgh Course in Applied Linguistics*. Vol. 3, (eds. Allen and Pit Corder).

Education Commission, 1964-66. Report.

Guerrini, M.C. 1986. Teaching Reported Speech. *English Teaching Forum*, Vol. XXIV, No. 2.

Gokak, V.K. Teaching People to teach others Well. *The Statesman*, Calcutta.

Hall, D.C. 1986. The VCR in the EFL Classroom. *English Teaching Forum*, Vol. XXIV, No. 2.

Hymes, D. 1972. On Communicative Competence. In : *Sociolinguistics* (ed. Pride and Holmes).

Johnson, K. 1982. *Communicative Syllabus Design and Methodology*. Pergamon.

Kennedy, C. 1979. Video in *ESP*. Journal of *ELT* (India), Vol. XIV, No. 6

Koul, B.N. 1975. *EST* and the Teacher of English in India. *CIEFL* Newsletter. No. 19.

Mathur, C.B. 1982. Teaching English and Skills Relevant to it. *The Journal of ELT* (India). Vol. XVII, No. 6.

Mohan, K. 1978. Imparting Communicative Competence. *The Journal of Language Education*, Ajmer: RCE.

Narayan, R.K. 1984 reprint. *The English Teacher,* Mysore : Indian Thought Publication,

Pattanayak, D.P. 1971. Teaching of Language Through Language Laboratories and Mass Media, *NIE Journal*, Vol. V, Nos. 5 and 6.

Pillai, S.S. 1979. Recent Trends to Communicative Approach to Teaching of ESP *Journal of ELT* (India), Vol. XIV, No. 5.

Prabhu, N.S. 1980. Theoretical Background to the Bangalore Project. *RIE* (South India) Bulletin, No. 4(1).

—.1982. The Communicational Teaching Project, South India. Paper presented at the TESOL Convention. Hawaii.

Press, John (ed.). 1963. *The Teaching of English Overseas*. London : Methuen Rai, U. 1983. English as she is taught. *Times of India*, New Delhi. November 8.

Rao, A.V.K. 1981. English for EST. *Journal of ELT* (India), Vol. XVI, No. 1.

Roberts, J.T. 1982. Recent Developments in *ELT Language Teaching Abstracts*. April and September.

Robinson, P. 1980. *ESP*. Oxford : Pergamon Press.

Roussel, F. 1983. Short Cuts to Communicative Competence. In : *Case Studies in ELT*. R.R. Jordan (Ed.) Collins.

Singh, R.K. 1982. *ESP* : A Sociolinguistic Consideration. *Journal of ELT* (India). Vol. XVII, No. 3.

Study Group. I & II—Reports.

Tosh, W. 1970. Computer Linguistics. In : *Linguistics*. A. Hall (Edit.). Madras : Higginbothams.

Widdowson, H.G. 1977. The Communicative Approach and its Application. *IJOAL*. New Delhi, Vol. III, No. 1.

—.1978. *Teaching Language as Communication*. OUP.

Wilkins, D.A. 1976. National Syllabuses. *OUP*.

Xavier, L. et. al. 1988. *Innovations in Indian ELT*. The Loyala Experiment. Loyala College, Madras.

3

"APPROPRIATE" ENGLISH LANGUAGE TEACHING TECHNOLOGY

A wide variety of ancillary teaching aids has been developed and many of them can be particularly helpful in teaching English in India as also in other developing areas. They can be used for several reasons, conscious and unconscious. They improve communication in the classroom, add to interest, relieve boredom, and increase the motivation of the students and teachers. It should be realised that effective learning is most likely to occur when educational opportunity coincides with vital daily concerns. A sincere attempt should be made to remove certain misconceptions about the utility of a number of these aids—that they are schoolish, are useful only to content-subject teachers, and are not usable with lecture techniques. Techniques for facilitating learning, remarks Strevens (1969), "can be very greatly improved by the use of appropriate aids and equipment". A. George ("An Enquiry into the Scope and Effectiveness of Audiovisual Instruction in Improving English Teaching in Kerala State"—Ph.D. Education, Kerala, 1966) enquired into the scope and effectiveness of audiovisual instruction in improving English teaching and found that the achievement of pupils taught by using audiovisual aids is greater than that of pupils taught by usual methods and that the use of audiovisual aids does not require more time than what is required for ordinary teaching. According to him, "Teachers did not use audiovisual aids because of heavy cost, heavy syllabus, insufficient number of material aids, and lack of skill and special training."

In addition to these aids, students should be encouraged to listen to the *B.B.C.* broadcasts, see good English films and study specimens, *e.g.*, coins, stamps, tickets, newspapers, and other paraphernalia, handy and small in size. These audiovisual materials are of different types ranging from teachers' notes and blackboards to language laboratories and computers. Some of the important types of aids are classroom equipment, printed and pictorial materials, projected materials, remote transmission media and materials, audio materials and multimedia packages, kits etc. A good teacher tends to be eclectic in his use of teaching aids and is resourceful enough to use them according to the circumstances.

Many of these aids are frightfully expensive from Indian standards. A computer has the capacity to store a vast amount of material and to present it in various audiovisual modes and can be programmed to test students, to keep a record of their progress, to point out their errors to them and to set remedial work. It may be noted here that though computer-assisted ELT is still in its infancy, the next few years may see interesting developments in this direction—if only foreign language teachers can learn the necessary programming skills. A revolution in the concept of teaching has been brought about by the introduction of multimedia instructional systems. In computer assisted instruction a student can choose his own pace and pause to test his comprehension. The computer guides him depending on his progress. On one side, the possibility of conducting a more intelligent dialogue with the student is being explored by providing screen-based learning to suit the liking of the student. On the other hand, efforts are being made to intermix full motion video and audio along with computer generated graphics, animation, simulation and text in a multimedia environment. In a multimedia courseware, the author can make use of full-motion video in a window of the computer screen to bring the real life processes before the student for indepth explanation and better comprehension.

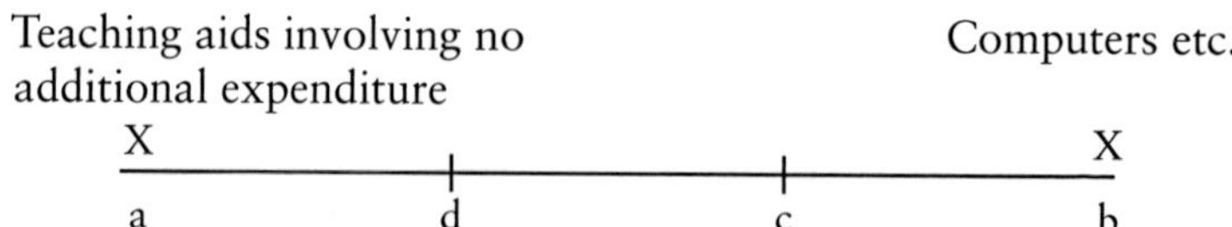

There is a big gap between these two extremes, 'a' and 'b'. So we must try to find a point of compromise. In the peculiar conditions prevailing in India it is necessary that the point should not be 'c' but d'. At the moment it would be more appropriate to locate that point somewhere between 'a' and 'd'. Undeniably, the shortage of funds and lack of technical knowledge act as barriers. Though, with the process of growth and social change, we are now finding more of better and well-equipped schools.

Simple, Capital-Saving Technology

In the Third World is imperative to use new aids of teaching in the classroom. The teaching of foreign languages in particular should not be a 'chalk and talk' profession only. But, at the same time, we cannot afford to be extravagant in this direction. Highly mechanized and electronically operated teaching aids will be difficult to manage particularly in rural areas. Instead of holding attention of the students of these areas such aids will perhaps make them nervous and unduly conscious. Expensive and sophisticated audiovisual aids, therefore, are no answer to our problem. They are suitable for utilization only on a limited scale and in selected places. How many full-fledged modern language laboratories have come up in India? Not many, perhaps, and even many teachers are not aware of the existence and use of such laboratories (on which alone it is estimated that over a million pounds was spent in Britain in five Years—Strevens : 1969), Even in Britain, however (as Strevens reported at the second International Congress of Applied Linguistics, September 1969) "administrators are beginning to ask questions which seem to them necessary in order to justify the now sizeable expenditure on aids and equipment for language teaching". Thus, we cannot recommend language laboratories, in these circumstances, for large scale use here. What is needed, therefore, is that we should devise simple, capital saving and more 'appropriate' technologies making full use of indigenous materials, and techniques appropriate to the needs of our country. Let no one carry the impression that when we plead for using 'appropriate' technology we play down the significance of big and capital intensive schemes. But it is also true that 'appropriate' technology is not an inferior technology; rather, it is the most useful one in the prevailing local conditions.

The charts 2 and 3 contain lists of selected audiovisual media. Most of them have been tested and found valuable in different parts of the world. But we in this country cannot make a free choice due to our limitations. Bearing in mind our characteristic requirements and genius we can however recommend puppetry and sand tables for wide use throughout the country besides blackboards, wall pictures, maps, plans, posters, charts, and models etc. Large pictures can be seen by the whole class by direct display and no projection is required.

Chart 1. Factors Influencing the Choice of Audiovisual Materials

1. Each of the following factors should be considered before the teacher makes a choice of audiovisual aids:

Pupil	T/L Situation			T/L Aims and Objectives		T/L Strategy
	Environment	Teacher	Economics	General Aims	Sequence Objective	T/L Steps
Age Socio-cultural background Sex Character motivation Previous experience: a. of the language b. of the course c. of media	Technical Physical conditions	Attitude Abilities Methods	Cost : to design to buy	Linguistic Cultural	A. Teaching 1. Productive or receptive skills: Speaking Listening Reading Writing 2. Cultural B. Testing	Recognition Repetition Reproduction Manipulation Production Presentation (general or selective context) Statement of Principle Mnemonics and Reinforcement Testing
All these factors affect design/choice/use of audiovisual aids.						The specific T/L step affects design/choice/ use of audiovisual aids

Adapted from Allen & Corder (Ed.) 1975.
Edinburgh Course in Applied
Linguistics, Vol. 3
pp. 267-8

Chart 2. Media an Design

Having considered all the above factcrs, the teacher is in a position to make a choice of audiovisual aids :

1. Basic Physical Requirements	Which Answer?	Medium	2. Pictorial Conversation	3. Audial Types of presentation
Visual				
big image/small image	1. Which medium?	Computer visual/	High Realism	Dramatic play with
for long range/short	2. Which visual	display TV (incl.	Selective	sound effects
range use	3. Which audial	(16 mm, 8 mm loop)	(simplified,	Dramatic Dialogue
single visual or part	type of	Film strip	expressive)	Interview
of sequence	presentation?	Slides	Stylization	Monologue
degree of ambiguity		Overhead Projector	Cartoon	Narration
permitted		Teaching Machines	Stereotype	Song-Poem
quantity of redundant		Posters	Pictograph	Monologue and/or
material permitted		Charts	Typeface	dialogue with
adaptable to various		Flashcards		fill in spaces.
T/L steps or not		Figurines		
technical ... of use		Readers		
movement		Workbooks		
3-dimensional form		Grammar Exercise Books		
colour, tone, line		Project Books		
composition, layout,		Kits		
stylistic character		Project Cards		
Audial		Games Cards		
degree of dramatic quality		Puppets Relia		
number of voices		Duplicator Radio		
quantity of sound effects		Records Tape		
need for interaction by pupil		Language Laboratory		

Adapted from Allen and Corder (Ed.) 1975. Edinburgh Course in Applied Linguistics. Vol. 3, pp. 267-8.

Chart 3. A Hierarchical Order of Selected Audiovisual Instrumental Media

Increasing prime cost (approximately) ↓ Difficulty of provision ↓ Generality ↓ Potential size of audience	Manuscript notes by lecturer or participant. Duplicated notes, bibliographies and references. Duplicated pictures — complete or with deliberate gaps Wall displays (including blackboard) Specimens (natural, *i.e.* real objects) Working models, formalized models, enlarged models, sandtables, puppetry. Epidiascopes Printed textbooks, work books Programmed sheet and books texts. Audio-tapes, local or general, discrecordings, Language laboratories (audio only) Skill slides, film strips, overhead projection. Audiovisual tutorials, augmented language laboratories Stereogram Moving overhead projection systems. Silent films, specially casetted loops. Sound films with magnetic (changeable) sound. Sound films with optical (built-in) sound. Programmed texts in machine formats. Radio-vision (broad cast sound plus in-house visuals). Video-tape recordings (CCTV) Audience-response systems Live TV programmes (CCTV) Computer-tested instructional system Sound broadcasts TV broadcasts	Increase in ease of use Ease of provision ↑ Specificity ↑ Cheapness

Adapted from D. Unwn (Ed.)
1969. *Media and Methods*, London,
McGraw Hill.

'Perforated' maps can be used for drawing. In a chart or picture the visual elements should be given precedence over words in conveying information. A complex story must be told in a series of pictures or charts. A new device—the felt board is very helpful in teaching stories and oral composition and another device, flash cards for teaching words and sentence structures. Models may be used if a teacher is unable to show the object directly. In the absence of picture and models the teacher can draw diagrams. A big calendar hanging in the class can be used to talk about the date and a clock-face with hands to talk about the time. The clock-face is helpful in teaching and practising the use of the past and future time references and a mirror in teaching pronunciation. Transparencies and colour slides can be used where facilities for using projected pictorial material exist. The visual memory, which is efficient and well-developed in all human beings, goes a long way in storing and retrieval of information and is more retentive. It is difficult to convey effectively all the relevant bits of information only through language. For teaching any language other than L_1, particularly the literature of the language, a good knowledge of its culture is necessary. Visual aids which are of great help in this grasp and experience of L_1 culture and also save explanation time. Frequently, pictures are used to establish the link between the concept-meaning and the word. They have been found very helpful in identifying object and feelings etc. and also for testing and exercising knowledge of words. They have been particularly useful for meaningful repetition and bringing home some grammatical rules more clearly. Wink (1978) has concentrated with remarkable success on the camping pictures available with W.R. Lee's Dolphin English Course. The English departments in schools and colleges should possess a library of informative and evocative pictures for the purposes of teaching. Simple cartoons or cartoon slides as supplement to normal class work can make the students realize the extended use of the second language.

Many advocate the value of drama for this purpose and have presented a language through drama (LTD) approach. The teacher asks students to work through a simple mime and then turns it into a vocal exercise. The students are asked to take the part of a burglar or thief getting into a house and then that of an old miser counting his money. In 'alphabet activities' the students are grouped in pairs and given a letter, such as 'A', and asked to devise a shared activity beginning with that letter. 'Starter cards' on which is written in print script a word such as LION or CAR; or on which is pasted a photograph of an object, a lock, a door or a book are given to group leaders (one card each group) who take their groups away to think of simple events on the basis of the object on the card. A few sentences can be, alternatively, printed to be used as the basis of a dramatic scene or dialogue. Certain communication situation—shop-keeper-customer situation, for instance—can be used as an exercise to encourage spontaneity of speech. Thus, different ploys like the story game and Snarl/Purr exercises can be used for this purpose. The singing of the songs reinforces teaching by helping to practise and revise vocabulary, idioms, sentence patterns, pronunciation, stress, rhythm and intonation in a variety of language styles. With the help of songs a teacher can change the pace of a classroom and thus can revive flagging attention. The teaching aids suggested by Rassias (1975) may be used not only in conversation classes, but also in grammar classes. Other media can be used at important centres where teachers also come for training.

We must now go on to discuss two of the 'appropriate' teaching aids, puppetry and sand tables, at some length.

Puppetry

Recently special attention has been paid to educational puppetry and it has been found valuable in a teaching situation. Literacy House, Lucknow, makes imaginative use of puppetry in its educational programmes. Indian puppeteers are popular for their skill and the government makes use of their shows for propaganda and publicity. When puppetry is used as a visual material in language teaching, the teacher has a greater control over content, timing and method. In fact, puppetry has the requisites to develop into a dvnamic teaching medium. If properly used, therefore, a puppet theatre can be an excellent piece of equipment in a second language classroom. Many years ago an experiment was conducted by the New York Board of Education to find out the utility of puppetry in the school to enrich the language aid programme. "It was found", says Currell (1969 : 11) "that, through puppetry, the children became aware of the importance of sequence in story-telling, they enriched their vocabularies, held discussions on the plot, script and production, and took an interest in classical music in order to find appropriate music for their plays ... There was evident eagerness to improve speech, and the problem children, finding that they were depended upon to do their share, did a good job". Currell adds, "this, however, is only a part of what can be achieved through puppetry". Sybil Marshall in her book, *An Experiment in Education*, has given a charming account of puppetry in her school. Currell has laid particular stress on staging puppet plays and telling stories through them.

Galarcep (1971) has recommended puppet shows as excellent audio-visual aids in the English class. Here are some of the ways in which, as Galarcep has recommended, puppets can be used in an English class :

1. to teach greetings
2. to teach prepositions
3. to teach comparatives and superlatives
4. to dramatise dialogues
5. in games
6. to present facts about nutrition
7. in rhythm studies
8. in biographies
9. in sketches.

For instance, we can teach prepositions with the help of a story or a game. Two puppets appear on the stage and move their hands to point different places.

Ram : I've lost my pencil, And I am sure you have it.

Zaid : Who? Me? I don't have it.

Ram : You have it under your coat (he lifts up Zaid's coat as if searching for it).

Zaid : No (he moves back). I saw it in Mohan's drawer. You must go into his bedroom.

Ram : (In the bedroom) Here it is, but on the table.

Zaid : Ram, have you found it?

Ram : Yes, but it wasn't in the drawer, it was on the table.

Remsbury (1972) finds puppetry of much use in language teaching by oral methods and lists the following as its practical advantages :

1. Puppets take the dullness out of repetition.
2. The puppet takes us out of the classroom.
3. 'Controlled conversations' go off with eclat.
4. Children remember a puppet show longer than a lesson: in this respect a puppet show is probably unrivalled by any other form of rural or visual aids.
5. There are no hurt feelings when a puppet criticises.

Experience has shown that since puppets have no "ego" they can be used to tackle more delicate subjects than live actors can.

Puppetry is of special benefit to shy and nervous children and also gives the feeling of involvement and participation to the entire class. These shows give a sense of relief from the tension of classroom teaching and add variety to the lesson. The use of puppetry as a teaching aid will also save time as time spent in going to the blackboard etc. is saved.

Puppets are convenient teaching aids also because they are easy, cheap and fascinating to prepare and can be taken anywhere and a show set up at a moment's notice. They can be made for a fraction of the cost of a tape recorder or overhead projector. It has been suggested that a spare-time puppet club can be established to fulfil the need of the schools for puppets. If necessary, these clubs can even put up puppet shows for recreation outside the class hours. Vocabulary tests arranged through puppetry will become interesting guessing games. Very useful counting games can also be arranged. Glove puppets or dolls can be used as talking partners in listening sessions. Olive Blackham and Helen Binyon demonstrated at the Bath Academy that the medium can also be utilised in teachers' training. It goes without saying, however, that one should be judicious and sparing in their use. If over-used they may become dull and uninteresting as tools of teaching.

We can make various types of puppets according to the requirements of the situation. Glove puppets with or without legs, papier mache puppets, rod puppets, wooden spoon puppets, articulated or non-articulated shadow puppets, the marionette with or without aeroplane control, tube puppets, padded cardboard puppets and simple wooden puppets are some of the more widely used puppets. The following is a diagram of a simple aeroplane control of the marionette. This puppet is worked by rocking the leg bar with a paddling movement.

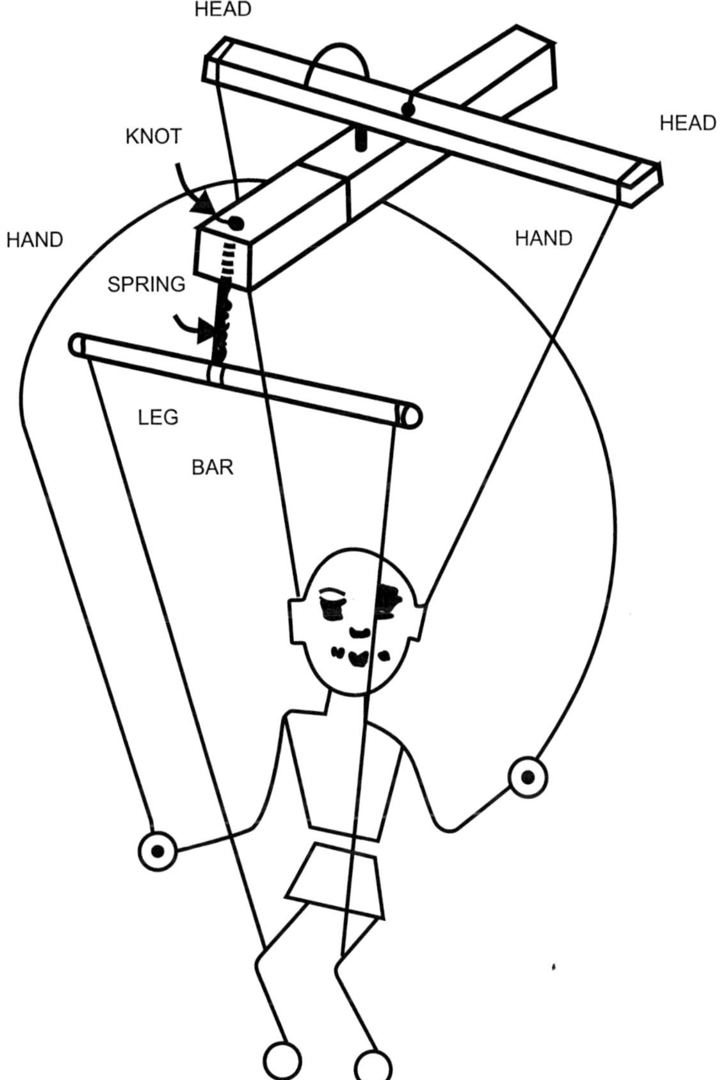

FIG. A SIMPLE AEROPLANE CONTROL OF THE MARIONETTE

The puppet should be dressed with soft materials before it is strung. A shadow puppet screen may be made from an old sheet. Though a theatre is not essential, a very simple and cheap, portable and multipurpose theatre has been designed and developed for such classroom shows.

Puppetry has been specially recommended for teaching immigrant children, handicapped children and also adolescents.

Sand Tables

Sand tables have been used to teach small children and also men in the army. Billows (1967 : 149) has mentioned a lesson in which he taught a prose passage to a linguistically very backward and tongue-tied fifth-year class of fourteen-and-fifteen-year-olds by means of a heap of sand he had made on the teacher's platform in front of the class. He was thus able to teach all the new vocabularly required by the piece. The students in mofussil areas in India are no better and that is why this aid is of special interest to us. Billows had taught the same piece with the help of simple sketches on the blackboard, but he found a clear advantage in working with actual materials, and having three dimensions instead of only two. It is thus possible to explain the situation and also to hold the attention of students. It is not too much to say that situations and words become one, and the students remember the scene. A notable merit of the sand-table is its transitoriness since the sand is immediately removed. Though the 'situation' is presented before the class it is also true that the whole thing is simply an 'approximation'. Something is left for the imagination which is thus made to work. As Billows remarks, "A sand table does not take the place of the imagination, or sidetrack it; it stimulates it."

It is so simple that a heap of sand on the floor, on the teacher's platform, or in a corner of the room has been found sufficient. It is also possible, however, to have a full-fledged sand table for this purpose. A simple table can be converted into a sand tabile by giving it a rim of cardboard. We can as well use a tray with or without legs. Other details like buildings etc. may be made of wood, cardboard or paper and may be used again and again from one landscape to another. Bushes and trees can be made of green tissue paper. The slopes of hills and fields can be coloured by sawdust. Blue sawdust can represent water. Shapes are to be moulded after dampening the sand. The models of seaside, countryside, island, town etc. can be arranged on sand-tables, or water-trays. With these background materials, we can talk about a large number of things in the classroom. These models indeed offer so much material for directed conversation practice. John and Frances Stoddart find the sand-table of remarkable use in the teaching of English to immigrant children.

The pupils recognise the sentences repeatedly used during the planning and making of new landscapes. As is the case with puppetry, a part of the work of moulding shapes out of slightly dampened sand may be done out of school to save time. In any case, however, a certain landscape should not be overused in the classroom as the students will naturally get bored with it.

The general point to be made, therefore, is that audio-visual teaching aids bring about motivation and the teaching of English becomes more successful and more rapid. The importance of the use of some cheap supporting materials in classrooms in India, therefore, cannot be overemphasized. The international conference on the teaching of English literature held at King's College, Cambridge, in 1962 (the recommendation holds good even now) had also noted that chief obstacles in underdeveloped area against applying audio-visual aids to the teaching of English are lack of funds, lack of facilities, and lack of technical resources, and that the teacher must improvise aids from whatever meagre resources may be near at hand. The use of audiov-isual aids must be limited by the economic resources of the country, and expenditure involved must always be taken into consideration. With this end in view, the present writer has recommended here some comparatively inexpensive and less complicated materials for wide use in this country. We can as well devise a number of other aids of like nature.

Application of Aids—A Challenge to the Teacher

It must be borne in mind that the application of these aids is not all that simple and the whole business is actually a clear challenge to the teacher. Sometimes the teacher may find the use of these techniques a little taxing. Of course, the teacher has to spend much time in gaining competence in the use of these materials. Nevertheless, it must be realized that they will ultimately prove beneficial to the teaching profession. If we seriously wish to improve the standards of language teaching in our country efforts must be made in the right earnest to spread their use. The teacher should see to it, however, that he does not over-use these aids. By giving extraordinary prominence to them the teacher might relegate the object to a position of secondary significance.

Though we have talked mainly about ELT the things said, we can reasonably claim, hold good for teaching in general. The aids suggested are, by and large, suitable for teaching several other subjects. The present writer has attempted to pinpoint a problem, an issue, and now he expects that the discussion here will give some food for thought to those working in the line. It is high time that they devote their attention to this aspect and point out or evolve technologies 'appropriate' for large scale use in the field of teaching in India.

REFERENCES

Allen and Corder (Ed.). 1975. Edinburgh Course in Applied Linguistics, Vol. 3.

Billows, F.L. 1967. The Techniques of Language Teaching. London : Longmans.

Bird, Alan. 1979. "The Use of Drama in Language Teaching". *English Language Teaching Journal*, Vol. XXXIII, No. 4.

Currell, D. 1969. *Puppetry in the Primary School*, London : Batsford.

Dutta, K.K. 1995. Blackboards on Computer. In : *The Telegraph*, Calcutta, January 10.

Literacy Discussion. 1972. International Institute for Adult Literacy Methods, Vol. III, No. 1.

Galarcep, F.M. 1971. "Puppets in Teaching English", *English Language Teaching Journal*, Vol. XXV, No. 2.

Nanda. V.S. March 1969. *Literacy on the Farm*. Span.

Rassias, J.L. 1975. "Teaching Aids", *IJOAL*, Vol. I, No. 2.

Rees, A.L.W. 1978. "Cartoon slides for the language class". *English Language Teaching Journal*, Vol. XXXII, No. 4.

—.1979, "Teachnique of presenting songs", *English Language Teaching Journal*, Vol. XXXI, No. 3.

Remsbury, Ann. 1972. "Oral Methods Through Puppetry", *English Language Teaching Journal*, Vol. XXVI, No. 3.

Roberts, J.T. 1982. Recent Developments in E.L.T. *Language Teaching Abstracts*, April and September.

Stoddart, John and Francis, 1968. The Teaching of English to Immigrant Children. London : University of London Press.

Strevens, P. 1969. "Where has all the money gone? The need for cost-effectiveness studies in the teaching of foreign languages". In: *Application of Linguistics*. 1971. Ed. G.E. Perren and J.L.M. Trim. Cambridge University Press.

Unwin, D. (ed.). 1969. *Media and Methods*, London: McGraw Hill.

Winks, M. 1978. "Using picture for oral composition". *English Language Teaching Journal*, Vol. XXXII, No. 4.

4

ENGLISH SPELLING – THE PROBLEMS OF INDIAN LEARNERS

In this chapter an attempt has been made to report on data pertaining to the approximate number of errors of spelling (in the English language) committed by the students of the matriculation class of a comparatively good school (run by the missionary) situated in the suburbs of a B class town in Eastern India. It is worth mentioning here that the types of errors the students of this school make are common to all schools in this area. The syllabus of English for the matriculation examination consists of a number of poems and prose pieces, two small books for non-detailed study and a full paper for composition. On passing the matriculation examination a student becomes eligible to join a college. 26 Pretest answer books each of 8 or 9 foolscap-sized pages formed the corpus. It was considered more useful to study long stretches of writing by a small number of students. Errors of spelling were collected from this corpus and then categorized.

Now, English language is a language of infinite difficulty in the matter of spelling. Interestingly, English spelling has been called a monument to traditionalism, so weird as to be practically incredible. Every word, according to Vallins (1954 : 304), is a law unto itself. Harold Palmer (1964 impression : 17) has pointed out that divergences (in English) from the actual language are so numerous and so great that we may be said to possess two distinct languages, the spoken and the written. The English spelling it not always a correct guide to the sounds the letters stand for. Some of the letters in the English alphabet are superfluous. One finds it rather difficult to agree with Sir Ifor Evans (1966 impression : 31) when he remarks that the difficulty of the spelling of English has been exaggerated (the present writer is not unaware of the historical reasons of the inconsistencies of English spelling) though, undeniably, some degree of predictability is there. Halliday, McIntosh and Strevens (1964 : 109) talk of the fierce resistance in Britain to any suggestions for spelling reform. "So strong is the feeling against it that it seems unlikely at present that any orthographic revision of English will be undertaken for a long time." "It has been said that for many learners, the sound-spelling system of English is highly 'demotivating and daunting'. At the same time, however, it has been widely recognised now that there is a great deal of regularity underlying the apparent chaos of English spelling."

Spelling has been quite a problem to Indian learners of English and, significantly, the problem has manifested itself in all its diversities in this study. The notorious difficulty of English spelling baffles and over-burdens our students who are, as is evident from this study, poor spellers.

Admittedly, the task of collecting and categorizing errors of spelling was not a simple one. The path was in fact bristling with many kinds of difficulties. To mention only one of them, there were many cases of combined errors. Consequently, a few overlappings and repetitions were unavoidable. Thus it would not be far too surprising if some readers branded as 'unhelpful' and 'unenlightening' the way errors have been categorized here. For instance, categorizing spellings such as 'fourty' as cases of the insertion of unnecessary vowel graphemes may be found as missing the point. Indisputably, however, this does not lessen the importance of the present study in any way nor does it make much of a difference with regard to the data collected.

Twenty-six answer books running into approximately 210 foolscap-sized pages yielded 1026 errors (of spelling) of different types. The highest number of errors that an answer book carried was 84 and the lowest 10 the average number of errors per answer book being 39.47.

The study reveals that vowels form the major source of difficulty. More than half of the total number of errors (56.35%) was connected with vowel graphemes (this figure does not include errors regarding vowels placed in other sections). Generally, Indian speakers of English do not place accent correctly and accent (for all we know) is the distinctive character of a vowel. It seems to be an easy guess, therefore, that students transfer their incorrect speech habits to writing—a fact which accounts for so many errors of spelling directly connected with vowel sounds *e.g.*, 'drainching'. 'thies', 'thoes', 'solt', 'boady', 'paints' (for 'pants'), 'sault', 'brek' (for 'break'), 'Hed' (for 'had'),

TABLE 1

Frequency distribution of errors

Type of error	Number	%
1. Errors connected with vowels	578	56.35
2. Errors connected with consonants	250	24.37
3. Errors connected with plural forms	18	1.75
4. Errors connected with past forms	15	1.46
5. Errors connected with proper names	30	2.92
6. Other errors (Difficult words, gross errors or errors due to hastle)	135	13.16
Total	1026	

'privet', 'cleaver', 'moderet', 'rad' (for 'red'), 'singal' (for 'single'), 'whiled' (for 'wheeled'), 'flad' (for 'fled'), 'attaintion' and 'seventin' etc. Long vowels have been shortened or made indistinct and monophthongs have been diphthongised. Since learners transfer their speech habits (which are generally habits of L_1), the problem of spelling is in a way a bilingual one.

TABLE 2

Frequency distribution of vowel errors

Type of error	Number	%
1. Replacement of vowel graphemes by other vowel graphemes	245	42.38
2. Double vowel graphemes singled	9	1.56
3. Single vowel grapheme doubled	3	0.51
4. Vowel graphemes transposed	19	3.29
5. Omission of vowel graphemes	202	34.95
6. Insertion of vowel graphemes not required	83	14.36
7. Vowel graphemes misplaced	17	2.94
Total	578	

Replacement of vowel graphemes by other vowel graphemes alone amounted to 245 errors (42.38% of the total number of errors regarding vowel graphemes).

TABLE 3

Frequency distribution of errors regarding replacement of vowel graphemes

Type of error	Number	%
e for a	28	11.43
u for a	2	0.82
e for i	12	4.90
u for eo	1	0.41
e for y	1	0.41
y for i	8	3.26
i for y	10	4.08
y for ie	2	0.82
y for e	3	1.22
a for ou	1	0.41
o for u	2	0.82
i for ea	7	2.86
ea for u	1	0.41
ea for i	4	1.63
a for e	34	13.88
i for a	17	6.94
a for i	7	2.86
o for a	37	15.10
o for e	1	0.41
u for i	4	1.63
u for e	8	3.26
a for o	6	2.45
e for o	2	0.82
io for ai	14	5.71
ea for ai	1	0.41
e for ai	1	0.41
i for e	18	7.35
a for u	6	2.45
ai for e	1	0.41
a for y	1	0.41
u for o	2	0.82
i for ee	3	1.22
Total	245	

Quite a few these may be assigned to the erroneous pronunciation of students *e.g.*, 'effection', 'gete', 'bedly', 'sleve', 'perents', 'petient'. 'et' (for 'at'), 'hunded' (for 'handed'), 'enymy', 'mordered', 'live' (for 'leave'), 'sit' (for 'seat'), 'bit' (for 'beat'), 'hips' (for 'heaps'), 'leave' (for 'live'), 'heat' (for 'hit'), 'naver' (for 'never'), 'famale', 'matel', 'exparienced', 'sattlement', 'tachnicians', 'wareless' (for 'wireless'), 'onother', 'laborotery', 'outo' (for 'auto'), 'drow' (for 'draw'), 'oll' (for 'all'), 'solt', 'shulter' (for 'shelter'), 'larry' (for 'lorry'), 'cangress', 'brether' (for 'brother'), 'caption' (for captain), 'mentain', and 'piped' (for 'peeped') etc. Many errors placed under this head reinforce our premise that students are perplexed by the nuances of English spelling. Some such errors are 'peculiar', 'villege', 'meny', 'eny', 'cheet', 'cheep', 'thousend', 'hether', 'thether', 'therty', 'surguns', 'banyans', 'historycal', 'beautyful', 'angri', 'parti', 'famili', 'carrys', 'jarney', 'daggar', 'collage', 'cought', 'rickshow', 'shurt', dancur', 'surgury', 'tharmal, 'travalling', 'anemy', 'experienced', 'anable', 'leathur', 'pawer', 'braught', 'visiter', 'intered', 'ingineer', 'rupies', 'sicret', 'passinger', 'intertainment', 'resirved', 'riporter', 'riturning', 'tarban', 'argent', 'woud' (for 'wood'), etc. In these cases the vowel graphemes are in fact replaceable without causing much harm to the sound. If 'many' is spelt 'meny' no damage is done to the sound though the spelling system is violently disturbed. The fact that pronunciation does not offer sufficient clue to the sound causes much bewilderment in the matter of spelling. English is not spelt as it is pronounced. Our schoolboys who are weak spellers easily become 'the dupe of unphonetic English spelling'. Often learners try to write exactly as the word is pronounced. Thus 'figure' is written 'figar' and 'operation' is made 'opration'. 'Dagger' has been written 'digger' seventeen times which is a very interesting instance of transferring wayward pronunciation to its equivalent written form. It should be remembered that some people pronounce 'dagger' as *daiger* in India.

There were 9 cases of using one vowel grapheme where two were required and 3 of using two vowel graphemes where only one was needed. Pronunciation of the words, once again, is one of the reasons of these errors, *e.g.*, 'to' (for 'too'), 'flor' (for 'floor'), 'shooes' (for 'shoes'), and 'pree' (for 'pre'). Sound plays a role of considerable significance in the transposition of vowel graphemes *e.g.*, 'theives' and 'cheif'.

TABLE 4

Frequency distribution of the transposition of vowel graphemes

Type of error	Number	%
ei made ie	1	5.26
ie made ei	16	84.21
ow made wo	1	5.26
ai made ie	1	5.26
Total	19	

Vowel graphemes have been omitted as many as 202 times (34.95%).

TABLE 5

Frequency distribution of omission of vowel graphemes

Type of error	Number	%
o omitted	15	7.43
i omitted	15	7.43
a omitted	25	12.38
e omitted	139	68.81
u omitted	8	3.96
Total	202	

Faulty pronunciation appears to be at the base of such errors as 'clour', 'possiblity', 'medicne', 'poltician', 'prepration', 'lether', 'enmy', 'ato' (for 'auto'), and 'montains', Vowel graphemes have been omitted in 'revison', 'transmisson', 'crimnals', 'suspicous', 'bord', 'secondry', 'helth', 'welth', 'deth', 'erly', 'colleg', 'dispensry', 'recived', 'belive', 'hight', brifly', 'opend', 'discoverd', 'joind', 'disguis', 'orderd', 'blu', 'killd', 'contry', 'hous', etc. chiefly because they could be dispensed with. 'Bombay' has been written once as 'Bomby' which is presumably a direct influence of L_1 (in many Indian languages 'Bombay' is called bʌmbəi:). Many Indians say *kəexri:d* (for 'carried') and *məeri: d* (for 'married'). Hence the errors. It is notable that 'e' has been left out no fewer than 50 times in writing the word 'thief'.

Insertion of vowel graphemes not required amounted to 83 errors (14.36%).

TABLE 6

Frequency distribution of insertion of vowel graphemes not required

Type of error	Number	%
o inserted	2	2.41
e inserted	46	55.42
u inserted	5	6.02
a inserted	20	24.09
i inserted	10	12.04
Total	83	

Ignorance has caused many of these errors though sound is also to blame. 'Catche', 'captaine', 'cooke', 'worke', 'maney', busey', and 'fourty' give us the sense the words stand for although misspelt because, largely speaking, the correct sound remains intact. The spelling of the words 'four' and 'fourteen' may be the reason for the occurrence of 'fourty'. Importantly, the grapheme 'e' has proved to be a problem grapheme. It was omitted 139 times and unnecessarily added on 46 occasions. 'e' at the end of the word has caused quite some anxiety. It has been omitted from the final position 37 times

TABLE 7

Frequency distribution of misplaced vowel graphemes

Type of error	Number	%
o misplaced	1	5.88
i misplaced	6	35.29
c misplaced	8	47.06
a misplaced	2	11.76
Total	17	

(*e.g.*, 'therefor', 'invit', 'mor', 'alon', 'opposit', 'colleg', 'wif', 'uncl', 'sincer', 'ther', 'rop' etc.) and has been wrongly inserted at the end 27 times (*e.g.*, 'shope', 'rede', 'dame' (for 'dam'), 'monthe', 'aske', 'rime' etc.). On 17 (2.94%) occasions vowel graphemes were misplaced.

Haste and imperfect knowledge have been responsible for these errors. 'Frist' and 'faimly' may have been written because of defective pronunciation and 'ocaison' and 'voilent' because these errors do not change the sound basically. Students found the use of 'ei' and 'ie' exceptionally embarrassing and thus made as may as 82 errors here. The following is the table of errors committed as a result of confusion in the use of 'ei' and 'ie' :

TABLE 8

Type of error	Number	%
i omitted	2	2.44
e omitted	62	75.64
ei transposed ie	1	2.22
ie transposed ei	16	19.52
y used instead of e	1	2.22
Total	82	

Another difficulty was noticed in the use of 'ea'—a difficulty which contributed 17 errors.

TABLE 9

Frequency distribution of errors in the use of 'ea'

Type of error	Number	%
a omitted	3	17.65
e omitted	2	11.76
i for ea	8	47.06
ea for u	1	5.88
ea for i	3	17.65
Total	17	

Two hundred fifty (24.37%) clear errors with regard to consonant graphemes were detected (exlcuding errors of consonant graphemes placed in other categories).

TABLE 10

Frequency distribution of errors regarding consonant graphemes

Type of error	Number	%
Replacement of consonant graphemes	41	16.4
Transposition of consonant graphemes	1	0.4
Omission of consonant graphemes	88	35.2
Single consonant grapheme doubled	45	18.0
Double consonant graphemes singled	56	22.4
Insertion of consonant graphemes not required	17	6.8
Consonant graphemes misplaced	2	0.8
Total	250	

Ignorance and wrong speech habits contribute to many of these errors. 'Britice', 'mistresh', 'forthy', 'dansh', 'pasent', 'bicked' (for 'wicked'), 'selter', 'sop', 'finised', 'Englis', 'sut', 'sake' (for 'shake'), 'sow' (for 'show'), 'sivering', 'mordern' etc. have been written primarily because of bad pronunciation. It is interesting to note that though in other sections errors with regard to consonant graphemes are far less than those related to vowel graphemes the consonant has outdone the vowel in respect of the singling of double consonant graphemes and doubling of single consonant graphemes. Undoubtedly, therefore, some confusion prevails in this area among learners. When 'thieff', 'addmission', 'boilling', 'proffessor', 'writting', 'autto', 'carefull' and 'dager', 'profesor', 'lory', lugage', 'oposite', 'realy', 'draged', and 'caried' are written errors of spelling are committed but not a marked alteration is rendered to the sound. It is obvious that 'full' is inserted in complete form in errors like 'carefull'. Many errors of consonant letters are really very abominable ones: no explanation can possibly be offered for them. This is particularly true about the omission of consonant graphemes which amounts to 86 (35.2%) errors. 'Atten' (for 'attend'), 'thanyou' (for 'thank you'), 'brough' (for 'brought'), 'passin' (for 'passing'), 'examinatio', 'prover' (for 'proverb'), 'achievent' (for 'achievement'), 'historica' (for 'historical'), 'tempe' (for 'temple'), 'clroth' (for 'cloth'), and 'reacherd' (for 'reached') deserve mention here. 'Exept' and 'frok' may have been written because 'c' in these words is not audibly pronounced. Some students have tried to reproduce faithfully the sound of words *e.g.*, 'sycle', 'persent', 'prise', 'danser' and 'danse' etc.

Eighteen errors (1.75%) related to plurals ('oxes', 'oxs', 'thiefes', 'leathers' etc.) were arranged together. 'Lariyan' and 'lariens' used as plural of 'lorry' are notable instances. There were 15 (1.46%) typical errors of past tense formation (this figure does not include errors of past tense discussed elsewhere). 'Brocked', 'hidded', 'choosed', 'droved', 'planded', 'drived', 'thinked', 'totaled' and 'starte' draw our attention. (It may be argued, however, that 'thinked' and 'drived' are not errors of spelling and that if these verbs were regular that would be their spelling.) Wrong spelling of proper names has added 30 (2.92%) to the total. 'St. Xavieas', 'Pantna', 'Afirica', 'Vanice' and 'Enland' etc. may be cited as examples.

On hundred thirtyfive errors (13.16%) were put in a different section which may be considered as a sort of miscellany. Errors which it was difficult to categorise otherwise (words with two or more errors or words written in a nonsensical manner rendering them meaningless) were placed here. Errors in this category may be called 'unsystematic' (as S. Pit Corder has done 1973 : 270). Errors like 'pode' (for 'poured'), 'bayristry', 'twestion' (for 'tuition'), 'enquestive', 'mattled' (for 'metalled'), and 'Eropians' may have been made since these words are understandably difficult ones considering the present day standards of matriculation students. Colossal ignorance, haste and carelessness have produced many of these errors. To mention some of them: 'readment' (for 'ready made'), 'complitly', 'lowers' (for 'lawyers'), 'lition' (for 'listen'), 'sicrete' (for 'secret'), 'celebression', 'bereck' (for 'barracks'), 'invait' (for 'invite') 'bissue' (for 'busy'), 'leat' (for 'late'), 'lari' (for 'lorry'), 'chop' (for 'chaff'), reconished' (for 'recognised'), 'sacrify' (for 'sacrifice'), thanku (for 'thank you'), 'animis' (for 'enemies'), 'cruwell' (for 'cruel'), 'simlilarly' (for 'similarly'), 'happing' (for 'happening'), 'predency' (for 'presidency'), 'comaman' (for 'common'), 'colthing' (for 'clothing'), 'dayagar' (for 'dagger'), 'rickow' (for 'rickshaw'), 'soaph' (for 'soap'), 'resurb' (for 'reserve'), 'dene' (for 'dinner'), and 'would' (for 'world'). Many errors in this list are ridiculous ones and make us laugh. In certain cases an absolutely different word has been written instead of the word needed *e.g.*, 'witch' (for 'which'). One has a feeling that with a slightly better knowledge and a little more of care many of these errors could have been avoided. Erratic pronunciation has led to errors like 'resurb', 'dayagar', mordon', and 'revait' (for 'rebate') etc.

Silent letters prove a stumbling block to learners of English as a second language. 'Recoding', 'shit' (for 'shirt'), 'paty' (for 'party'), 'foty' (for 'forty'), 'hadly' (for 'hardly'), 'britely' (for 'brightly'), and 'no' (for 'know') are clear instances. It is this problem which has contributed so many errors pertaining to 'e' in the final position (omission where required and addition where not required). The silent 'e' was not inserted in many past forms ('killd', 'joind' and 'orderd'). Sounds 's' and 'sh' have caused a great deal of trouble (*e.g.*, 'sop' for 'shop' and 'closhed' for 'closed').

Though not considered errors for present purposes wrong splittings of words have also been noticed *e.g.*, 'to morrow', "out side', 'respect fully', 'fire wood', 'mid night', 'there fore', 'fore noon', etc. Erroneous shortening has resulted in a number of errors *e.g.*, 'examina'. It should be emphasized here that a comparatively high number of errors were committed by examinees while translating the passage from L_1 into English. Inconsistency was frequently in evidence. Sometimes the same word was spelt correctly on one occasion and incorrectly on the other by the same student—the student is obviously passing through 'the practice stage of learning.' Though very occasionally, Americanisms were also encountered during this study *e.g.*, 'program'. 'Their' and 'there' were frequently confused. At times the spelling of the word was quite in order though situation demanded the use of a different word or the same word with a different inflection—'covertly erroneous' uses. The following are some relevant examples :

(i) we shall bath
(ii) many nurse and doctor
(iii) to came down
(iv) to made
(v) a oil
(vi) his brother take
(vii) After pass the examination

Conclusion

Major sources of these errors:

(1) Ignorance on the part of learners.
(2) Improper and deficient drilling of the spelling in the classroom.
(3) 'Untidinesses' and 'inconsistencies' of English spelling.
(4) Erroneous pronunciation of learners—speech habits deficient in many ways (with reference to English).
(5) Inaccurate placing of the accent by learners.
(6) Habit of spelling the word exactly as the word is spoken—'pronunciation spelling'.
(7) Interference of the mother tongue.
(8) Haste and carelessness.
(9) Overgeneralization of the rules of forming plurals and past tense.
(10) Imperfect sense of proper names.
(11) Difficult words (for the matriculation standard).
(12) False analogy—'principled but incorrect guesses.'

Suggestions

(1) Spelling drill—with special stress on the particular part of the word found difficult by the pupil—Transcription—Insertion of missing letters.

(2) Habits of correct pronunciation to be imbibed—no misrepresentation of consonants.

(3) Proper placing of the accent—particular care of vowel sounds.

(4) A list be made of words (or sound sequences) in respect of which greater number of errors are detected *e.g.*, the list prepared by the present writer.

(5) Some classes of errors can be guarded against by rules.

(6) To eschew haste and carelessness.

(7) Drilling in respect of plural and past forms.

(8) Visual memory be stressed and developed.

REFERENCES

Evans, Sir B. Ifor. 1966. *The Use of English*, London & Guildford: Macgibbon and Kee.

Halliday, M.A.K., McIntosh A. and Strevens P. 1964. *The Linguistic Sciences and language Teaching*, London : Longmans.

Palmer, H.E. 1964. *The Principles of Language Study*, London : OUP.

Pit Corder, S. 1973. *Introducing Applied Linguistics*, Panguin Education.

Vallins, G.H. 1954. *Spelling*. Andre Deutsch.

5

THE ARTICLE – A PROBLEM FOR THE UNDERGRADUATE STUDENT IN INDIA

The users of English Language and particularly those for whom it is a second language often go wrong in respect of the proper use of articles—articles are misplaced, omitted where necessary and inserted where they are not required. This study was undertaken with a view to collecting relevant data to ascertain the approximate number and nature of mistakes of articles made by Indian undergraduate students.

REVIEW OF LITERATURE

(A short note on the article)

Time was (it is claimed) when the English language had no articles. 'A' and 'an' are said to be developed short forms of 'one' and 'the' that of old English 'this' and 'that'. It is thought that weak forms emerged as Zipf's law (that human beings want to economize physically) worked.

The monosyllables 'a' or 'an' and 'the' are usually referred to as 'articles'. Jacobs and Rosenbaum (1968 : 44) talk of *these* as well as *this, that*, and *those*, as "demonstrative" articles. They are also called 'determiners' and according to this logic, should be placed within the nominal group 'modifier', as has been done by Caroll (1971). "Determiners pattern like 'the' ", says Berkoff (1966 : 15). But, whereas all 'articles' are 'determiners', all 'determiners' cannot be labelled as articles'. 'Some', for example, is a determiner though not an article. It is interesting to note that Strang (1968 : 202) has discussed 'some' as a non-definite article in the plural form (example: some books). It would be interesting to distinguish between the stressed 'some'/S∧m/as definite and the unstressed /sm/or/s∂m/as non-definite. To mention incidentally,

Ona Low (1966 : 20) has cited cases wherein the use of the definite articles with an uncountable noun may suggest 'all', its omission 'some' (ex. 1. He gave information to the enemy. 2. He gave the information of the enemy). Jespersen's (1969 : 161) statement about the definite article deserves notice : "As *the* is phonetically a weaker *that*, its meaning also is weakened: instead of pointing out it serves to designate or single out. *The* is generally called the definite article: a better name would be the defining or determining article. It has really two distinct functions, that of determining in itself, and that of determining in connexion with a following word or words containing the essential specification. We therefore speak of *the article of complete and the article of incomplete determination.*" Since transformationalists prefer to narrow down the scope of adjectives they have introduced a "separate category" for determiners. The system of determiners has been divided into three sub-classes: (1) regular determiners; (2) post-determiners; and (3) predeterminers. Articles fall under regular determiners which occur before nouns. Thomas (1970 : 80) has placed 'any', 'every' and 'some' under articles. Sometimes the definite article is separated from its noun by one or more other words: 'the last student', the most dependable friend'. 'Noun-phrase initiators' is the name given to pre-articles by Strang (1968 : 132). *All* (generally 'all does not precede the indefinite article: exception in earlier English—all a summer's day'), *both*, *half* are important instances. Thus a determiner can also be re-written as (Pre-article) + Art. Other pre-articles are 'several of' and 'many of' Thomas (1970 : 84) draws our attention to the fact that the predeterminers are invariably separated from the regular determiners by the word *of*. Thomas considers of—in this case—to be a special morpheme: the predeterminer morpheme. Strang (1968 : 127-128) has mentioned two more articles, 'negative' articles and 'genitive' articles. She links *no* with the articles "in the sense that the three form a mutually exclusive system (no one head can have more than one as adjunct), and in the sense that it shares their special position in the noun-phrase—indeed, not even the two forms that can precede the other two can precede it....It is a noun-phrase negator in "No really sweet and sound eating apples have been available all the week...when it does function in the noun-phrase it is so like the articles that we may call it the negative article". Strang (1968 : 128) goes on to point out that the forms *my, our, you, her, their,* and marginally *his, its*— pattern like determiners and more specifically like articles. "They form a system mutually exclusive with the other article (we cannot say 'the my apple' etc.), they share the special position of articles in the noun-phrase, being preceded only by the noun-phrase initiators (as in 'our lovely new house' but 'all our yesterdays'). For these reasons it seems best to class these words as *genitive articles*, some central because like true articles they have no other sentence—function and so signal the onset of noun-phrases, others (*his, its*) marginal because they do have another function." Though the present writer considers some of these pronouncements quite courageous, he will confine himself in this study to the traditionally recognised articles.

Sanderson (1966 : 198) has observed with reference to the article, "with an open ear and eye for examples to copy, and no panic, or taking things for granted, the main uses are not too hard to pick up, and do not always disagree strongly with use of article in your own language (if any)". The article is available in the Indo-European language, some big African language groups and many other languages. Generally speaking, 'article' is a word with the noun or a form of the noun and is used to indicate singularity, vagueness, and definiteness. In fact articles are important determiners since they are markers of the following noun : it shows the very nounness of its headword. Thomas (1970 : 80) gives a rule which says that every noun in English is preceded by a regular determiner of some sort—certain nouns are generally preceded by the Zero article. As Sweet put it in 1876 (In *The English Language*, Vol. 2, Boulton and Crystal, 1969 : 21), "any part of speech may be made into a noun simply by prefixing an article or adjective".

A remarkable feature of the article is that it is lexically empty though it contributes to the meaning of the headword as a noun. The absence of the article is sometimes referred to as the Zero-form. Sweet (p. 11) asserted that though the articles had an unmistakable but somewhat vague meaning of their own the two syllables (*a* and *the*) would convey no meaning if pronounced alone. Interestingly, Sweet (p. 12) has compared the meaning of deprivation and negation in the *de* of *deny* and *depose* with the generalising and specifying meaning of the prefixes in 'a man' and 'the man'. He has also compared the meaninglessness of the English articles ('they amount practically to nothing more than prefixes for forming nouns') with the definite articles in French and German and feels that there is a greater lexical emptiness in the latter (p. 25).

Sweet (p. 12) has raised a question whether 'the man' or 'a man' is one word or two words. Then he finds a way out and calls 'man' a full-word and 'the' a half-word—that is a word incapable of forming a sentence by itself, or of suggesting an independent meaning. According to Bloomfield a free form could be recognised by its ability to stand as a complete utterance. But these articles can make complete statements only in a context of language, not of life. Therefore, Burgess (In *The English Language*, Ed. Boulton and Crystal : 1969 : 297) is of the view that we must regard the articles as bound forms—forms incapable of acting on their own—that is to say, not as words at all. But in fact the articles are regarded as words; they have space before and behind. Burgess suggests that "we allow the morpheme in its two forms—the morpheme expressing meaning; the morpheme which merely helps to modify meaning or create larger structures—to rest as our scientific unit."

Lately there has been a notable laxity in the use of the article—particularly the definite article (specially when the individualization is self-evident). Barber (1964 : 179) remarks, "It is also possible that changes are taking place in the use of the definite article: it is very often omitted in positions where it would formerly have been normal." However, he says, a little later, "It is difficult to say whether such changes are going to have any long-term significance." Nevertheless article—deletion is quite obvious in space—saving telegraphic English and classified ads. The tendency to ignore the articles in modern English is noticeably active—Krishnaswamy also subscribes to this view in his article "Grammar, old and new", *NIE Journal*, January '71. The use of the definite article is more sparing in English than in many other languages whereas the use of the indefinite article is less restricted.

MATERIALS AND METHODS

The experiment was conducted in a degree college situated in a sub-divisional town some 25 miles from district headquarters—centre of a full-fledged modern university. The II-year Arts students of that college were asked to write a very brief essay on the topic of their choice and, significantly, they chose to write on "The Cow". The students concerned were not allowed to consult any books or notes. Thus 35 specimen answers were collected. The average number of words used by them was around 100. These specimen essays were closely examined and the mistakes of article underlined.

They were collected and placed under different heads. Thus it was possible to come to certain conclusions in this regard. In fact, the essays were generally full of very bad mistakes—often the sentences were semantically vague and syntactically defective. That is why the effort in this work was found bristling with difficulties. Many a time it was difficult to pinpoint the type of error as the sentences did not make much sense and also there were very many other errors around. In such cases the present writer had to depend on his discretion. Hence the figures thus collected should be taken only as approximate ones. It is also significant that the answers were written without preparation. No notice in this connection was given to them in advance. In certain sentences this writer had to make some corrections to make them look sensible (but without affecting the error in the use of article).

FINDINGS AND DISCUSSION

(a) Omission of 'a'

This amounted to the maximum number of errors. Out of a total of 92 errors 29 were of this type, which comes to 31.50%. It seems that this is so chiefly because many students literally translate the Hindi version into English. In most of the Indian languages the indefinite article (specially the classifying use of it) is not used to the extent it is used in English. A number of answers contained constructions like 'The cow is four footed animal' and that she 'has long tail' and 'big neck'. The source of this error can be easily traced in the mother tongue where *gai chaupaya jaanwar hae* is a normal statement and not *gai ek chaupaaya janwar hae.* In much the same way students are accustomed to saying in their mother tongue sentences like *gai ko dum hoti hae* and *gai ko lambi gardan hoti hae* and that is why when they write this type of statement in English they are content with the exact equivalents and ignore 'a' as it is not thought necessary. Really the indefinite article in such expressions acts as hindrance chiefly because of L_1 interference.

(b) Omission of 'the'

There were 26 omissions of the definite article which amounted to 28.29% of the total. This error should be ascribed once again to L_1 interference, though to a lesser degree. For instance *gai hame doodh deti hae* is translated as 'cow gives us milk'. There were 20 omissions of 'the' before 'cow' and 2 before 'calf' although in each case students named the species in general. A particular answer carried 3 such omissions.

(c) Insertion of the definite article where not required

Bracketed with the omission of 'the' was the insertion of 'the' where not required. 'The' was inserted unnecessarily in 26 positions *i.e.*, 28.29% of the total number of errors. Students placed 'the' before words like 'many', proper noun like 'India', before countable plurals and unspecified nouns. Perhaps students were slightly confused in respect of the use of the definite article as they were apparently unable to decide where to insert it and where to omit; and that made them place it in positions where it was not required. This writer will hold L_1 partially responsible for it, once again.

(d) Insertion of the indefinite article where not required

There were two cases of the constructions like 'The cow is a very useful for me' and one of 'The cow is domestic an animal' (Is this student under the impression that 'an' precedes every word beginning with a vowel sound? One construction is Hindus call it as a Gau Mata'). 'She gives us a calf, and 'she gives us a skin' are the two sentences with which some people might find not much of a fault but I have, however, preferred to place them among the wrong and not among the acceptable ones. Obviously L_1 plays a role in these mistakes as well. Only 7 out of 92 mistakes fall under this head.

(e) 'a' instead of 'the'

There was only one clear mistake of this type when a student wrote 'a best manure' whereas actually the superlative is preceded by 'the' and not 'a'. Importantly, a certain student has written the following four sentences:

(i) A cow is loved by all.

(ii) A cow has many colours.

(iii) A cow eats grass.

(iv) A cow gives calf.

It is true that when a single example is preceded by indefinite article it may represent a whole group, yet, perhaps, it is more appropriate to use 'the' in such cases, for the sake of clarity and uniformity. But, of course, I do not list the above four sentences among wrong ones.

Since there is only one mistake each of inserting 'a' instead of 'an' ('The cow is a animal') and 'an' instead of 'a' ('an domestic animal') it can be presumed that students largely follow the necessary rule. Likewise only one mistake of placing 'the' instead of 'a' could be located ('... which is the very important thing') which is negligible.

TABLE 1

Sl. No.	Types of mistake	Number of mistakes	Percentage with references to the total number of mistakes
1.	Omission of 'a'	29	31.50%
2.	Omission of 'the'	26	28.29%
3.	Insertion of 'the' where not required	26	28.29%
4.	'a' or 'an' not required	7	7.60%
5.	'a' instead of 'an'	1	1.08%
6.	'a' instead of 'the'	1	1.08%
7.	'an' instead of 'a'	1	1.08%
8.	'the' instead of 'a'	1	1.08%
	Total	92	

Conclusion

About 3,000 words written by 35 students contained 92 clear mistakes of articles, which is quite on the high side. However, the fact that these answers were written by the students of a college situated in the suburbs or mofussil area of a town, a college where merit is not much of a consideration in admissions and where most of the students are tribals should not be lost sight of. Answers written were generally poor and that makes the data thus obtained representative of standards on the lower side.

Omission of 'the' where required and its insertion where not required taken together amounted to more than half of the errors *i.e.*, 56.58%. Thus the study reveals that students find the definite article particularly confusing. Individually, omission of 'a' heads the list with 31.50%. The blame for this can be placed almost squarely on L_1 interference. It is noteworthy that a particular answer contained 5 omissions of 'a' and the same answer contained two omissions of 'the'. There were 12 other answers having both these omissions. These figures indicate some kind of link between these two kinds of omissions. The indefinite article is incorrectly inserted in 7 positions. Mistakes of other types were very few in number and were not of much consequence and a few of them may have occurred through slip or oversight.

TABLE 2

Number of mistakes	Number of answers	Percentage with reference to the total number of answers
0	2	5.71%
1	10	28.57%
2	8	22.85%
3	4	11.42%
4	7	20.00%
5	1	2.85%
6	1	2.85%
7	1	2.85%
8	1	2.85%
9	0	0%

That students often make mistakes in respect of proper placing of the article is apparent from the study and it would be in the fitness of things to say that the article comes as a clear hindrance in learning English as L_2. L_1 interference, as has been noted earlier is the major source of these mistakes. To be exact there is no article worthy of the name in Indian languages though it may be said that Hindi/e i K/has two functions—the numeral function and the article function. To some extent, the same is true of/*v*əh/. Hence students find themselves at a loss in this area. Thomas (1970 : 87) has also remarked : "Some speakers for whom English is a second language have considerable difficulty with the English determiner system particularly when their own language lacks article." One of the reasons of why so many mistakes of this type are committed is that students go in for a translation of the thought in largely a literal style. We might guess that had these articles carried some meaning they would not have caused such a large number of mistakes. Articles are, however, devoid of any meaning and this meaninglessness also, perhaps, causes these mistakes.

It should not be too much to say that students do not know much about the article. The present writer wanted to know from the students who wrote the answers considered in this study as to what they knew about the article. It is revealing that they avoided the question and were reluctant to say anything.

Some of the mistakes were naturally made through carelessness and haste. It is important, however, that a little more of carelessness is discernible in connection with the article. It is commonly believed in a section that the article is not a very significant part of grammar and thus does not deserve much attention. Indeed, it is as important as any other part of grammar. Lexically, too, it often assumes a vital position and its presence of absence can change the meaning.

The present writer would suggest that some more attention be paid to this branch of grammar in schools. We should let the students know the significance of articles in English (even if the significance is of a minor nature) as distinguished from Indian languages where they are mostly absent.

REFERENCES

Barber, Chales. 1964. *Linguistic Change in Present Day English*, Edinburgh and London.

Berkoff, N.A. 1966. *English Structures and Exercises*, London: Allman & Sons.

Burgess, Anthony. 1964. In : *The English Language*, Vol. 2, 1969. Selected and edited by Boulton and Crystal, Cambridge University Press.

Caroll, B.J. 1971. *Systems and Structures of English*, Madras : OUP.

Jacobs & Rosenbaum. 1968. *English Transformational Grammar*, Blaistell International Edition.

Jespersen, Otto. 1969. *Essentials of English Grammar*, London.

Low, Ona. 1966. *Certificate of Proficiency English Course for Foreign Students*, London.

Sanderson, P. 1966. *Key English*, Perganon Press.

Strang, Barbara M.H. 1968. *Modern English Structure*, London.

Sweet, Henry. 1876. "Words, Logic and Grammar". In : *The English Language*, Vol. 2, *op. cit.*

Thomas, Owen, 1970. *Transformational Grammar and the Teacher of English*. Holt International Edition.

6

SCHOOL FINAL STUDENTS AND THE USE OF PREPOSITION

The preposition, as a matter of fact, accounts for a pretty large number of common errors. Right at the outset it should be conceded, however, that the correct and proper use of prepositions is not verv easy either. Even Close (1962 : 142) finds many usages "very difficult to systematise. This is not surprising. Some of the relationships we want to express are very complex. We express them by little words whose full meaning could only be explained in circumlocutions. Moreover, the number of these little words is limited, and each may have to serve a variety of purposes." Close has also emphasized that "great many usages can only be mastered by mechanical associations...in some of these purely mechanical associations even native-English usage can be uncertain and conflicting". Thus it is not unnatural that the students who learn English as L_2 find this area bristling with difficulties. The purpose of this study was to categorize the common errors of preposition committed by the students of Class XI—candidates for matriculation. The findings are presented in this paper.

It would not be irrelevant to mention here that a student of Class XI in India has to study several short poems, prose pieces, and one or two supplementary books as rapid reading. There is a full paper for composition also wherein essay-writing, letter-writing, translation into English from the mother tongue etc. are prescribed. Immediately after passing the matriculation examination the students go to college. The main significance of this study lies in the fact that through it, we know the state of affairs obtaining in a typical school at a time when the students concerned are just on the threshold of university education.

The students of Class XI of a good missionary school situated near a big town—divisional headquarters, were given 15 sentences, each with a blank, and were asked to fill them up with 'appropriate' prepositions. Mostly lower middle class and working class children belonging to different linguistic backgrounds come to this school and they are not much exposed to English. This school has reasonably sufficient educational facilities. A total of 35 students of the age group of 14-17 who were present in the class participated. Much emphasis was laid on the 'appropriateness' of the prepositions to be supplied. Perhaps some blanks could have been filled up by some other prepositions as well but only the 'appropriate' ones were taken as correct (and this by no means makes the test ambiguous). This stress on 'appropriateness' was announced to the class in advance. It is essential that the students should know the appropriate places where the particular prepositions should be used.

The following were the sentences given to the students for the test :

TABLE 1

S. No.	Sentences	'Appropriate' Prepositions
1.	The teacher is angry — me.	with
2.	He is always — your service.	at
3.	Jaunpur is famous — its perfumes.	for
4.	Your opinion is different — mine.	from
5.	I congratulate you — your success.	on
6.	He presided — the meeting.	over
7.	He deals — rice.	in
8.	I prefer reading—writing.	to
9.	He stood — me in my distress.	by
10.	He was accused — theft.	of
11.	They have entered — an agreement.	into
12.	Protect yourself — dangers.	against
13.	It has to be divided — Ram and Shyam.	between
14.	Please distribute these books — five students.	among
15.	I enquired of Ram — Harihar's house.	about

It is true that the sentences chosen were not very simple ones. But it must be borne in mind that the school achieved about 95%

success in the last matriculation (annual) examination. Also, the teacher who teaches English claimed that all this was taught to the class. Importantly, most of the sentences were borrowed from the question papers of the previous years.

There were in total 525 blanks to be filled in (15 each by 35 students) with 'appropriate' prepositions and 375 errors were committed, *i.e.*, 71.43%. Six blanks left untouched have also been considered errors. The highest number of errors in an answer was 13 and as many as 8 out of 35 answers had 13 errors whereas only 2 contained the lowest number of errors *i.e.*, 7. It is significant that no answer was without error.

TABLE 2

Frequency of errors	Number of answers	%
1	Zero	0
2	Zero	0
3	Zero	0
4	Zero	0
5	Zero	0
6	Zero	0
7	2	5.71
8	2	5.71
9	6	17.14
10	6	17.14
11	5	14.29
12	6	17.14
13	8	22.86
14	Zero	0
15	Zero	0
Total	35	

Table 2 shows that the number of errors ranged from 7 to 13 which speaks for itself. It should be noted that only 2 answers had 7 and 2 others 8 errors. Other answers carried higher number of errors.

TABLE 3

Distribution of the Errors of Preposition

Serial No.	'Appropriate' Preposition	Number of errors	%
1.	'With'	01	0.27
2.	'At'	35	9.33
3.	'For'	16	4.27
4.	'From'	14	3.73
5.	'On'	21	5.60
6.	'Over'	35	9.33
7.	'In'	23	6.13
8.	'To'	19	5.07
9.	'By'	34	9.07
10.	'Of'	23	6.13
11.	'Into'	29	7.73
12.	'Against'	35	9.33
13.	'Between'	32	8.53
14.	'Among'	29	7.73
15.	'About'	29	7.73
Total		375	

Table 3 shows the distribution of errors relating to the 15 prepositions. Now, let us take up each of these 15 prepositions and the errors in connection with them.

With (0.27%) : Very surprisingly there was only one error here when a student wrote 'upon' instead of 'with'. 'With' indeed appears to be a class apart. The students largely know the rules with regard to its proper use.

At (9.33%) : The result here also springs a surprise as no student could place 'at' correctly. 28.57% wrote 'to' instead of 'at', 20.00% 'in' and 17.14% 'on'. 'In the service' is a proper use and thus 'in' here may have been used due to over-generalization. 'At' and 'in' are easily confused. 'In' and 'on' were perhaps placed as the English equivalents of the proper Hindi usage. Use of 'to' is more surprising than the use of 'on' or 'in' because with 'on' or 'in' the sentence does not lose much in meaning.

For (4.27%) : The result with regard to 'for' is comparatively satisfying. It seems it is so chiefly because the sentence given called for almost an exact translation of Hindi and Urdu *ke liye*. Insertion of 'of' instead of 'for' constitutes the bulk (68.75%) here though it is, once again, surprising as with 'of' the sentence does not make any sense.

From (3.73%) : It seems the students are by and large familiar with the proper use of 'from' as a preposition as only 3.73% have committed errors. The use of 'with' instead of 'from' in such constructions is a common error and hence 28.57% placed 'with'. It is amazing to realize, however, that the same number of students have placed 'of'.

On (5.60%) : The task of the students in respect of 'on' was somewhat easy as 'to congratulate on success' is a common use but 5.60% committed error. 28.57% used 'for' instead of 'on' which is, once again, a common error: many people wrongly use 'for' for 'on' in such cases. 19.05% used 'upon' which is also understandable but 'in' has been used by 19.05% perhaps under the influence of the mother tongue, Hindi or Urdu.

Over (9.33%) : The result here has been disastrous : no answer was correct. Instead of 'over', 40.00% placed 'to' which may have been due to misunderstanding of the meaning of the sentence. 28.86% used 'in' and 11.42% 'at'. The interference caused by the mother tongue (Hindi or Urdu) perhaps resulted in the use of 'in' and 'at' since in Hindi and Urdu many say *jalse meN*. With 'in' and 'at' the sentence conveys some meaning as well.

In (6.13%), 34.78% have used 'to' instead of 'in' which I guess is the result of semantic confusion. 17.39% who have placed 'with' have perhaps confused the use here with the well-known phrase 'to deal with'. The use of 'of' amounts to the same percentage of errors.

To (5.07%) : 'To' is a very common preposition and the result with regard to 'to' has also been comparatively encouraging. 47.37% have, however, placed 'with' instead of 'to' and with 'with' also the sentence becomes meaningful. 21.05% have placed 'and' and 5.26% 'or'. Though the mistakes here ('and' and 'or') are quite serious the fact remains that 'and' and 'or' make the sentence somehow meaningful.

By (9.07%) : 'By' proved to be another problem preposition as only one student used it correctly. 35.21% used 'with' instead of 'by' taking that the sentence would be 'He stood *with* me in my distress'. 8.82% preferred 'beside' which also gives some meaning to the sentence.

Of (6.13%) : As 'of' is a widely used preposition and the sentence given was also a comparatively straightforward one, it accounts for only 6.13% of errors. Confusion in the sense here made 30.43% use 'by' and 21.74% who have used 'for' and 8.69% who have used 'in', it can be presumed, were confused.

Into (7.73%) : The use of 'in' by 31.03% and of 'to' by 20.69% is understandable. Admittedly, 'in' and 'into' are easily confused. Generally, the students are not very clear about the proper use of 'into' which is composed of two simple prepositions.

Against (9.33%) : Undeniably, the students found the use of 'against' quite baffling. There was no correct answer and, revealingly, 11.42% left the blank untouched, 20.00% used 'from' which is a common error but 34.28% placed 'of' which appears difficult to explain. But those who used 'of' were obviously ignorant of the word 'protect'.

Between (8.53%) : This preposition was also found difficult. The use of 'by' for 'between' amounts to the largest number of errors here and with 'by' too, the sentence does not lose sense.

Among (7.73%) : 41.38% have placed 'in' for 'among' which is not a rare sight. 17.24% have used 'between' which is also a common error. Perhaps with 'into' (6.89%) also the students could make out some meaning from the sentence.

About (7.73%) : 41.38% have used 'from' perhaps because 'from' also imparts meaning to the sentence. The same can be said about those (13.79%) who have opted for 'in'. Unintelligent carelessness, it can be presumed, has made 20.69% use 'with'.

Indisputably, the students find this part of grammar quite baffling. Thomas (1970 : 200) has drawn our attention towards the difficulty in this sphere and has noted that a detailed analysis of English prepositions does not exist. Pittman (1967 : 16) observes about prepositions, "These small words, so small that it is easy to overlook them, all have many, many meanings. *Of* has sixty-three meanings listed in the *Oxford English Dictionary* and other prepositions have almost as many meanings."

It seems that often in a state of sheer confusion the boys just place any of the prepositions and usually the results in such cases are ridiculous. Apparently, in filling the blanks with 'appropriate' prepositions the main objective of the students is simply to make out some sort of sense from the sentence. For instance, when one says/writes, "I am always on/in your service" it is not that the listener/reader does not get the sense though 'on' and 'in' are not 'grammatical' here. But many students, it seems, feel that their task is accomplished the moment they can deduce some meaning from the sentence. Most of the errors can be attributed to this approach. Another major cause is that the students decide in favour of a certain preposition on account of analogy (which is perhaps a major factor in the misuse of prepositions). 'He is in the house' is grammatical and, therefore, by way of analogy, the blank in the sentence No. 15 has been filled with 'in' by 4 students: presumably, they rationalize a deviant usage bearing in mind their previous experience of English. The mother tongue also acts as a barrier and is an important source of these errors *e.g.*, the use of 'for' instead of 'on' in the sentence No. 5 can be ascribed to the inter-language (Hindi-Urdu-English) interference. Hindi was the mother tongue of 19 students in the class and Urdu of 4. The problems of the Hindi and Urdu speaking students are quite identical. But among the tribal students the mother tongue of 4 was Mundari and of 5 Oraon whereas 1 tribal student had Santhali as his mother tongue. For the tribal students the problem is, in fact, twofold. From their mother tongue (L_1) they come to Hindi (L_2) and only then go to English which is actually L_3 for them. It is notable that when we study the linguistic backgrounds of the students we come to interesting conclusions. Hindi is, in fact, almost as foreign to an Oraon or Mundari speaking student as English. They are quite different languages: Oraon belongs to the Dravidian group of languages whereas Hindi is an Indo-European language. The Bengali-speaking students (who numbered two) face an absolutely different kind of interference.

The students found 'at', 'over' and 'against' particularly difficult. Surprisingly enough, no student has placed them correctly although at least 'at' is a very common and widely used preposition. 'By', with only one correct answer, has also been equally problematic. The result with regard to 'with' (0.27%) has been unexpectedly good. Only one student did not place 'with' in "The teacher is angry— me". 'For', 'from' and 'to' (4.27%, 3.73% and 5.07%, respectively) have also proved popular with the students. Those who have come forward with non-prepositions (in the blanks), perhaps, do not know much about prepositions.

Since prepositions form a significant part of grammar students should try to be as clear about them as they can and teachers should also thoroughly examine their teaching materials. Intensive oral drills with particular regard to the use of appropriate prepositions should be of help because mechanical associations play an important role here. It is true that these errors can be remedied if efforts are made in the right direction though, as we have noted, even native-English usage can be uncertain and conflicting in this area. The nature of these errors often indicates that not much work is done in the class in this respect. According to Pittman (1967 : 98), "early in our English course, the teaching of the common prepositions *of, to, from, on, at, in, into, for, with, by*, will provide plenty of brightness in our lessons, for these words are easy to teach in their common concrete meanings. Oral drill is very easy to obtain with a few common objects used one after another". However, it is by ample reading, writing, listening, and speaking that one gets a clear idea of the correct use of prepositions.

REFERENCES

Close, R A. 1962. *English as a Foreign Language*, London: George Allen and Unwin Ltd.

Pittman, G.A. 1967. *Teaching Structural English*, London : Ginn and Co.

Thomas, Owen. 1970. *Transformational Grammar and the Teacher of English*, A Holt International Edition.

APPENDIX

Tables I – XV – Errors pertaining to the 15 prepositions.

Serial No.	Type of error	Number	%

TABLE I

'*WITH*'

Serial No.	Type of error	Number	%
1.	'Upon' instead of 'with'	1	0.27

TABLE II

'*AT*'

Serial No.	Type of error	Number	%
1.	'In' instead of 'at'	7	20.00
2.	'Of' instead of 'at'	1	2.86
3.	'On' instead of 'at'	6	17.14
4.	'To' instead of 'at'	10	28.56

Serial No.	Type of error	Number	%
5.	'Upon' instead of 'at'	3	8.57
6.	'For' instead of 'at'	4	11.43
7.	'With' instead of 'at'	1	2.86
Misc.			
8.	'Do' instead of 'at'	2	5.71
9.	Left blank	1	2.86
	Total	35	

TABLE III

'FOR'			
1.	'Of' instead of 'for'	11	68.75
2.	'To' instead of 'for'	2	12.50
3.	'In' instead of 'for'	2	12.50
4.	'With' instead of 'for'	1	6.25
	Total	16	

TABLE IV

'FROM'			
1.	'At' instead of 'from'	2	14.29
2.	'With' instead of 'from'	4	28.57
3.	'Of' instead of 'from'	4	28.57
4.	'In' instead of 'from'	1	7.14
5.	'For' instead of 'from'	2	14.29
6.	'Between' instead of 'from'	1	7.14
	Total	14	

TABLE V

'ON'			
1.	'For' instead of 'on'	6	28.57
2.	'Upon' instead of 'on'	4	19.05
3.	'From' instead of 'on'	2	9.52
4.	'In' instead of 'on'	4	19.05
5.	'To' instead of 'on'	3	14.29
6.	'With' instead of 'on'	1	4.76

Serial No.	Type of error	Number	%
Misc.			
7.	'Or' instead of 'on'	1	4.76
		Total 21	

TABLE VI

Serial No.	Type of error	Number	%
'OVER'			
1.	'To' instead of 'over'	14	40.00
2.	'In' instead of 'over'	8	22.86
3.	'Up' instead of 'over'	6	17.14
4.	'At' instead of 'over'	4	11.42
5.	'For' instead of 'over'	1	2.86
6.	'On' instead of 'over'	1	2.86
Misc			
7.	'That' instead of 'over'	1	2.86
		Total 35	

TABLE VII

Serial No.	Type of error	Number	%
'IN'			
1.	'With' instead of 'in'	4	17.39
2.	'At' instead of 'in'	1	4.35
3.	'To' instead of 'in'	8	34.78
4.	'On' instead of 'in'	3	13.04
5.	'Of' instead of 'in'	4	17.39
6.	'For' instead of 'in'	2	8.69
Misc.			
7.	'Him' instead of 'in'	1	4.35
		Total 23	

TABLE VIII

Serial No.	Type of error	Number	%
'TO'			
1.	'With' instead of 'to'	9	47.37
2.	'For' instead of 'to'	2	1053
3.	'In' instead of 'to'	1	5.26
4.	'On' instead of 'to'	1	5.26

Serial No.	Type of error	Number	%
Misc.			
5.	'And' instead of 'to'	4	21.05
6.	'Or' instead of 'to'	1	5.26
7.	'The' instead of 'to'	1	5.26
		Total 19	

TABLE IX

	'BY'		
1.	'With' instead of 'by'	12	35.29
2.	'At' instead of 'by'	1	2.94
3.	'To' instead of 'by'	7	20.59
4.	'Upon' instead of 'by'	4	11.77
5.	'Up' instead of 'by'	2	5.88
6.	'On' instead of 'by'	2	5.88
7.	'For' instead of 'by'	1	2.94
8.	'From' instead of 'by'	1	2.94
9.	'Beside' instead of 'by'	3	8.82
Misc.			
10.	Left blank	1	2.94
		Total 34	

TABLE X

	'OF'		
1.	'In' instead of 'of'	2	8.69
2.	'By' instead of 'of'	7	30.43
3.	'To' instead of 'of'	4	17.39
4.	'For' instead of 'of'	5	21.74
5.	'With' instead of 'of'	1	4.35
6.	'Upon instead of 'of'	1	4.35
7.	'From' instead of 'of'	1	4.35

Serial No.	Type of error	Number	%
Misc.			
8.	'Often' instead of 'of'	1	4.35
9.	'Your' instead of 'of'	1	4.35
		Total 23	

TABLE XI

'INTO'			
1.	'With' instead of 'into'	6	20.69
2.	'At' instead of 'into'	1	3.45
3.	'In' instead of 'into'	9	31.03
4.	'To' instead of 'into'	6	20.69
5.	'From' instead of 'into'	2	6.89
6.	'Of' instead of 'into'	1	3.45
7.	'For' instead of 'into'	2	6.89
8.	'On' instead of 'into'	1	3.45
Misc.			
9.	'It' instead of 'into'	1	3.45
		Total 29	

TABLE XII

'AGAINST'			
1.	'Of' instead of 'against'	12	34.28
2.	'In' instead of 'against'	6	17.14
3.	'Upon' instead of 'against'	1	2.86
4.	'On' instead of 'against'	1	2.86
5.	'From' instead of 'against'	7	20.00
6.	'For' instead of 'against'	1	2.86
7.	'By' instead of 'against'	1	2.86
8.	'To' instead of 'against'	1	2.86
9.	'With' instead of 'against'	1	2.86
Misc.			
10.	Left blank	4	11.42
		Total 35	

Serial No.	Type of error	Number	%

TABLE XIII

Serial No.	Type of error	Number	%
'BETWEEN'			
1.	'Into' instead of 'between'	2	6.25
2.	'At' instead of 'between'	1	3.12
3.	'For' instead of 'between'	1	3.12
4.	'From' instead of 'between'	3	9.38
5.	'Of' instead of 'between'	3	9.38
6.	'By' instead of 'between'	7	21.88
7.	'With' instead of 'between'	3	9.38
8.	'Among' instead of 'between'	5	15.63
9.	'To' instead of 'between'	2	6.25
10.	'In' instead of 'between'	2	6.25
11.	'On' instead of 'between'	1	3.12
12.	'Up' instead of 'between'	1	3.12
Misc.			
13.	'Was' instead of 'between'	1	3.12
	Total	32	

TABLE XIV

Serial No.	Type of error	Number	%
'AMONG'			
1.	'In' instead of 'among'	12	41.38
2.	'Of' instead of 'among'	2	6.89
3.	'By' instead of 'among'	2	6.89
4.	'To' instead of 'among'	1	3.45
5.	'Between' instead of 'among'	5	17.24
6.	'On' instead of 'among'	1	3.45
7.	'For' instead of 'among'	3	10.35
8.	'Into' instead of 'among'	2	6.89
9.	'Up' instead of 'among'	1	3.45
	Total	29	

TABLE XV

Serial No.	Type of error	Number	%
'ABOUT'			
1.	'In' instead of 'about'	4	13.79
2.	'At' instead of 'about'	1	3.45
3.	'With' instead of 'about'	6	20.69
4.	'Of' instead of 'about'	1	3.45
5.	'From' instead of 'about'	12	41.38
6.	'Among' instead of 'about'	1	3.45
7.	'For' instead of 'about'	1	3.45
8.	'To' instead of 'about'	1	3.45
Misc.			
9.	'And' instead of 'about'	2	6.89
	Total	29	

7

THE PREPOSITION AND THE UNDERGRADUATE

This chapter deals with data with regard to the approximate number of errors in the use of prepositions committed by the Intermediate (Science) students (of the age group of 16-18) in writing essays. The data presented here indicate the exact nature of the deficiencies and difficulties of these students in this area. This study also brings to the fore how the students fare in the college with the passage of time since an attempt has been made to compare the errors in the answer books of the first and second terminal examinations of the same students.

The essays in 19 answer books of the first terminal examination held soon after the students had joined college and were fresh from schools, were taken up for a close scrutiny. The clear errors in the use of prepositions were marked, collected, and categorized. Then the essays in the answer books of the second terminal examination of the same examinees were subjected to minute analysis and the errors of preposition were, once again, underlined and placed under different heads. It should be noted that there was a gap of 7 months between the two examinations. The experiment was conducted in the premier institution of a university. The examinees came mostly from middle class families. Some of them have passed out from the English medium schools. 3 or 4 of them belong to the scheduled tribes for whom English is not L_2 but L_3 or L_4—their multi-lingualism sometimes acts as a barrier in learning English. It is true that the types of errors the students of this college make are common to all colleges of this area. The first terminal examination was held when the students concerned were in the first year science class and the second took place when they were already second year science students. The average length of the essays was 2 foolscap-sized pages.

Indisputably, prepositions enable the users of English to express themselves accurately and are an important part of the English grammar. Many writers including Vallins (1955 : 37) have warned against any false economy in respect of their use. We agree with Pittman (1967 : 10) when he says that though prepositions are easy to teach at elementary level, they are perhaps the most difficult to teach at advanced level. This view in particular increases the significance of the present investigation.

The inquiry has revealed certain kinds of errors of preposition which deserve close analysis. It is hoped that the results will be of interest to the teachers of English as a foreign language elsewhere too. Such analyses, in fact, enable the teachers to go to the level of students themselves and to have a look at the students' difficulties from the students' own standpoints and thus to find out the areas where they need special help.

In the first terminal examination the 19 essays contained 111 clear errors of preposition. Some 7 months later things had only slightly improved since the essays written by the same 19 students in the second terminal examination had 100 errors only. This by no means indicates a very satisfactory state of affairs and undoubtedly there is room for improvement. The comparatively short essays contained fewer errors but it is noteworthy that when the same students wrote longer essays in the second terminal examination they committed more errors. It would not be too much to say that some students become idle and just let things happen and, as a result, they deteriorate. A comparative study of the results in respect of the two terminal examinations gives interesting and meaningful conclusions. Out of 19 students 9 improved, 7 deteriorated, and there was no change in 3 of them. This once again gives us food for thought. It is really a serious matter why 7 students out of 19 committed more errors later when they should have actually improved. The question that arises here is as to why the students are unable to learn.

It is found that in many cases prepositions were omitted the omission of prepositions amounted to 28.80% of errors in the first terminal examination and the number went down to 25% in the second. It is evident thus that there is a general tendency among students to omit prepositions. Another notable tendency is to insert them where they are not required. This also accounts for a pretty large number of errors. Insertion of prepositions where they were not required caused 19.80% errors in the first terminal examination. The position with regard to them was found slightly improved in the second terminal examination where such insertions accounted for 19% errors.

50.40% errors in the first terminal examination were caused by (it can be guessed) confusion—one preposition used instead of the other. 54% errors were caused by confusion of this nature in the second terminal examination.

The inquiry reveals that as a general rule students do not use many prepositions : they use only a limited number of the more common among them. Here they have confined themselves to 14 prepositions ('To', 'In', 'With', 'At', 'By', 'For', 'Of, 'On', 'Upon', 'From', 'Till', 'Among', 'About' and 'After'). It is so largely because their vocabulary is comparatively small and they avoid big and complicated structures. For instance (a digression may be permitted here) they display an obvious predilection for writing sentences in simple present tense and try to avoid sentences with past and future time references perhaps because they find the latter comparatively difficult.

There are certain pairs of preposition which are easily confused. 'At' and 'In' make one such pair. The confusion about them is quite common. In this study 'in' used for 'at' caused 6.30% errors in the first terminal examination and 7% in the second whereas 'at' used for 'in' resulted in 4.50% errors in the first terminal examination and 4% in the second.

'To' and 'in' have been found to be comparatively 'popular' with the examinees : these prepositions get the lion's share of errors. 'To' has been found to be particularly confusing. It is omitted where required in 9.00% cases in the first terminal and 7% in the second. The insertion of 'to' where it was not required resulted in 9.90% errors in the first terminal examination and 10% in the second. In the first terminal examination the confusion in the proper use of 'to' amounted to 27.90% errors and this confusion caused 24% errors in the second. The use of prepositions is, in fact, not found all that simple by those students whose L_1 is either Hindi or Urdu (most of the examinees studied here had Hindi as L_1). For example, the Hindi or Urdu translation of the English sentence 'He went to London' will not have any equivalent to the preposition 'to'. Consequently, the errors with regard to 'to' predominate. The errors with regard to the use of 'in' were 23.40% in the first terminal examination and 27% in the second. 'At' gets the third position with 8.10% and 12% errors in the first and second terminal examinations respectively: 'for' is a close fourth. There is only one error each of 'upon' and 'after' in the first terminal examination and none in the second. It should not be supposed, however, that the students are quite familiar with the proper use of these prepositions. The fact is that they do not use them frequently enough and show a typical tendency, as emphasized earlier, to restrict themselves to common and simple prepositions only (*e.g.*, 'to' and 'in') while writing.

Frequently the construction of the sentences was such as to make the task of locating and pinpointing the error of preposition difficult (though such sentences were semantically incongruous or absurd). Thus most of the sentences cited as examples here have not been considered as having the errors of preposition for the purpose of the data.

It is learnt from this study that the students cannot use with felicity the structures involving uses like 'in pulling' and 'in completing' etc. They rather prefer to say "He spends his life to pull the rickshaw" and "They are interested to see cinema". Sometimes, as one gathers, wrong constructions of the sentences make them place the preposition irregularly. Some typical sentences (from the examination answers) are :

— "There is no arrangement for teaching his children."
— "to earn money to fulfilment".
— "This amount is not satisfied to him".
— "He sleeps with hunger."
— "in the last time".
— "They check every student with clever."
— "In this season the sunlight is very effected to human being."

Occasionally, the idioms containing these prepositions are not used appropriately and thus confusion is caused :

— "They look at very beautiful."
— "They put on the chits from their pockets".

— "The people are dying shortage of food".

— "They do not look after him with respect".

At times peculiar situations are created because these prepositions are wrongly placed :

— "The programme is declared before two weeks".

— "I gave to answer every question".

— "Some students come in late examination hall".

It would be relevant to point out here that the syllabuses are not primarily language-oriented and the methods used to teach the poems and stories prescribed are generally not effective in respect of language teaching. The findings of this inquiry should persuade us to examine our teaching materials and sincere attempts should be made to make them suitable and appropriate for the pupils concerned. It is good for teachers to acquaint themselves with the kind of errors their students make. The pupils should be given sufficient practice in using the prepositions. It is advisable to give intensive drills in different structures where some confusion prevails. Since the errors reported in this study have been committed by college students who have, in theory at least, received instruction on all these items, re-teaching may prove effective. The teachers should bear in mind the pupils' particular deficiencies and requirements. Systematic drills will definitely help a great deal in such cases. It is also necessary that the pupils should know what is wrong with the forms they have used. We hope that this will make them think and thus the learning of the correct forms will be facilitated. However, it must also be emphasized that the use of many of these prepositions can be mastered chiefly by intelligent manipulation of mechanical associations.

REFERENCES

Pittman, G.A. 1969. *Teaching Structural English*, London : Ginn & Co.

Vallins, G.H. 1955. *Better English*, Andre Deutsch Ltd.

APPENDIX

Tables I – IV

I – List of Errors

Sl. No.	Error	% error	
		First Terminal Examination	Second Terminal Examination
(1)	(2)	(3)	(4)
1.	'With' not required	0.90	–
2.	'With' for 'from'	0.90	1
3.	'With'omitted	0.90	–
4.	'With' for 'by'	–	3
5.	'With' for 'to'	–	1
6.	'In' omitted	4.51	7
7.	'In' for 'at'	6.31	7
8.	'In' not required	3.60	2
9.	'In' for 'for'	0.90	1
10.	'In' for 'between'	0.90	–
11.	'In' for 'on'	6.31	6
12.	'In' for 'to'	0.90	2
13.	'In' for 'with'	–	1
14.	'In' for 'of'	–	1
15.	'At' omitted	1.80	4
16.	'At' not required	0.90	1
17.	'At' for 'in'	4.51	4
18.	'At' for 'from'	0.90	–
19.	'At' for 'on'	–	3
20.	'To' for 'in'	3.60	1
21.	'To' omitted	9.01	7
22.	'To' not required	9.91	10
23.	'To' for 'by'	1.80	–
24.	'To' for 'with'	0.90	–

(1)	(2)	(3)	(4)
25.	'To' for 'for'	–	1
26.	'To' for 'of'	–	3
27.	'To' for 'from'	2.70	2
28.	'By' omitted	1.80	–
29.	'By' for 'with'	0.90	1
30.	'By' not required	0.90	–
31.	'By' for 'for'	0.90	–
32.	'By' for 'in'	–	1
33.	'For' not required	1.80	–
34.	'For' omitted	2.70	3
35.	'For' for 'to'	2.70	3
36.	'For' for 'of'	0.90	1
37.	'For' for 'on'	–	1
38.	'Of' not required	1.80	4
39.	'Of' omitted	0.90	3
40.	'Of' for 'to'	0.90	2
41.	'Of' for 'from'	–	1
42.	'Of' for 'in'	–	2
43.	'On' for 'for'	0.90	–
44.	'On' for 'of'	0.90	–
45.	'On' omitted	1.80	–
46.	'On' for 'by'	0.90	–
47.	'On' for 'in'	2.70	4
48.	'On' for 'at'	0.90	–
49.	'Upon' for 'by'	0.90	–
50.	'From' omitted	3.60	–
51.	'From' for 'to'	0.90	–
52.	'From' for 'of'	–	3
53.	'From' not reqired	–	2
54.	'Till' for 'for'	0.90	–
55.	'Among' omitted	1.80	1
56.	'About' for 'for'	1.80	–
57.	'After' for 'for'	0.90	–
58.	'Is' for 'in'	2.70	–

II – Number of Errors-Comparison

Specimen No.	Number of errors: First Terminal Examination	Number of errors: Second Terminal Examination	Remarks
1.	4	4	No change
2.	2	8	Deteriorated
3.	8	8	No change
4.	2	1	Improved
5.	11	15	Deteriorated
6.	5	11	Deteriorated
7.	7	1	Improved
8.	7	2	Improved
9.	10	7	Improved
10.	5	8	Deteriorated
11.	3	4	Deteriorated
12.	2	1	Improved
13.	10	7	Improved
14.	2	3	Deteriorated
15.	5	3	Improved
16.	16	6	Improved
17.	7	4	Improved
18.	4	6	Deteriorated
19.	1	1	No change
Total	111	100	

III – Prepositions Omitted

Preposition	% First Terminal Examination	% Second Terminal Examination
'With'	.90	–
'In'	4.50	7
'At'	1.80	4
'To'	9.00	7
'By'	1.80	–

'For'	2.70	3
'Of'	.90	3
'On'	1.80	–
'From'	3.60	–
'Among'	1.80	1
Total	28.80	25

IV – Prepositions Inserted where not required

Preposition	%	
	First Terminal Examination	Second Terminal Examination
'With'	.90	–
'In'	3.60	2
'At'	.90	1
'To'	9.90	10
'By'	.90	–
'For'	1.80	–
'Of'	1.80	4
'From'	–	2
Total	19.80	19

8

REMEDYING ERRORS

Linguistic approaches to errors are Contrastive analysis (CA) approach and error analysis (EA) approach. People who have worked in this field disagree on how far they should go to claim for interlingual interference the most significant place among the types of errors. French (1963 impression : 7) says: "Thus in seeking the source of error in the vernacular the teacher is searching in the wrong field." Also, contrastive analysis cannot predict all the areas of difficulties and some of its predictions may not prove true at all. At the same time, L_1 interference is only one of the sources of errors. But the fact remains that one of the variables that lead to success or failure in language learning is the conflict between linguistic systems and that is why with the help of CA we come to certain definite conclusions with regard to the real source of errors. If a Hindi speaking student comes out with *I wented there yesterday* it is unquestionably not the L_1 that is causing the error but English. In all probability, the student produces *wented* on the analogy of *wanted.* The approach of the error analysts therefore is an attempt in the direction of dealing with the practical requirements of the classroom teacher. It goes without saying that EA has a great feedback value with regard to designing instructional materials and determining strategies. E.A. can reveal both the 'success' and 'failures' of the teaching programme itself. Proper remedial measures can thus be devised and employed both to consolidate the 'successes' and to eliminate the 'failures'. This approach does not restrict the analysis to errors caused only by the gravitational pull of the mother tongue. EA can test the prediction and supplement the results of CA. Sharma (1980) thinks that 'the mother tongue background is felt ominously all through error analysis'. To be true, we do not feel like agreeing with Candler (1979) when he says that

EA focuses attention on trivial aspects of language learning. In fact, EA has been a great contribution of applied linguistics. Lee (1965) has stressed that EA may influence the order in which vocabulary is introduced—"Mistakes in the use of sounds, words, and structures may thus be usefully collected and examined, and mistakes analysis at each of these levels can be applied to language teaching. Through the examination of learners' mistakes a teacher may enter more fully into the environment of teaching and put on, as it were, his pupils' linguistic spectacles". It should be stressed here that L_1 also facilitates the learning of L_2—a case of this nature is one of positive transfer. Nöth (1979) talks of a linguistics of errors analysing all forms of deviant language behaviour. This new branch of linguistics is concerned with errors deriving from different causes. Thus, he asserts, there are two different types of linguistic analyses relevant to error analysis: monosystematic and dia-systematic language analysis. Errors which can be located within a single system of language are the subject of a monosystematic analysis. The typical errors of performance like the slips in speaking, reading and writing belong to this type of analysis. The dia-systematic analysis treats errors which are caused by the interference between several language systems. Nöth talks of error linguistics, error evaluation and error therapy. Many researchers have pleaded for an integrated approach to EA. Such an integrated approach should (i) identify the errors made by learners, (ii) describe them in linguistic terms, (iii) explain their sources, and (iv) suggest which rules of grammar and usage should be established to help the learners overcome these errors.

It should be realized that a student who has committed errors needs a training in using the rules of grammar 'unconsciously'. A contextualised exercise is therefore always more useful and rewarding. A combination of rules and practice will be particularly helpful. At any rate, the exercises should not become monotonous. The various kinds of drills may be used, substitution drills—situational and semi-situational drills and transformation drills etc.

The frequency counts of errors enable the classroom teacher to decide which errors are to be taken seriously and, therefore, to be given priority. The learning strategy has to he chosen accordingly. It would be reasonable to consider EA a form of self-education. However, a suggestion has been made recently that we need not be very strict in marking these errors. It has been said that Indian students are being penalized in tests and examinations for saying and writing things which educated Englishmen are permitted to say all the time. Those who argue in favour of this approach plead for a more liberal attitude to errors. It is true that there are obvious limitations in the ability of any individual in analyzing deviant language behaviour or errors because more than one form may be acceptable. Indeed, 'errors only' approach is not something commendable. In fact, teachers' attitudes towards learners' errors have in recent years become more tolerant.

Interlanguage

Larry Selinker's paper 'Interlanguage' was begun during the 1968-69 academic year while he was at the Department of Applied Linguistics, University of Edinburgh. An earlier version of the paper was presented at the second International Congress of Applied Linguistics, Cambridge University, 1969. A revised version of the paper was published in IRAL (International Review of Applied Linguistics, Vol. X/3, 1972).

Selinker focuses on the psychological aspects of L_2 learning. He asserts that the data on which theories of L_2 learning should be based must be the learner's real or attempted communication in the second language. The main point of interest here is Selinker's typology or classification of attempted learning, resulting in an interlanguage. The interlanguage is, in fact, a different language system from either the mother tongue or the target language. The successive linguistic systems that a learner constructs on his way to mastery in a target language has been called Interlanguage by Selinker. "The interlanguage is said to constitute a dynamic linguistic application of rules, strategies and hypotheses"—(Richards and Kennedy : 1977). These systems have been referred to as Idiosyncratic Dialects by S. Pit Corder and Approximative Systems by Nemser. However, the term 'interlanguage' is being widely used these days perhaps because of its neutrality. Obviously, it does not give a TL centred perspective. Sridhar (1976) finds the term appropriate also for the following reasons:

(i) it captures the indeterminate status of the learner's systems between his NL and the TL.

(ii) it represents the "atypical rapidity" with which the learner's language changes, or its instability.

(iii) focusing on the term language, it emphatically recognizes the rule-governed, systematic nature of the learner's performance and its inadequacy as a functional communicative system (from the learner's point of view, at least).

According to Selinker himself this paper is written from the learning perspective, regardless of one's failure or success in the attempted learning of L_2. The notable influence on the study of interlanguage phenomena has been the findings of the studies of child language acquisition. It has been found that the current approach considers child language learning as a progression of self-contained, internally structured systems, getting increasingly closer to the adult language system. Jakobson advocated the same approach as early as 1941. He stresses the notion that a child's language is always a coherent system (although with more marginal features and fluctuations than adult language). He is also of the view that the development of child's language may profitably be regarded as succession of stages. There is an obvious parallelism between this change of approach in developmental psycholinguistics and the change from the traditional error analysis to the concept of Interlanguage.

Importantly, Selinker has given a theoretical framework in order to account for the IL (interlanguage) phenomena in L_2 learning. He is of the opinion that L_2 learning theories should be based on the learner's communication in the target language. In a given situation the utterances made by the learner are different from those a native speaker would produce in the same situation. That is why, Selinker remarks that "one would be completely justified in hypothesizing, perhaps even compelled to hypothesize, the existence of a separate linguistic system based on the observable output which results from a learner's attempted production of a target language norm. This linguistic system he calls interlanguage. The important thing here is Selinker's belief in the existence of a psychological structure latent in the brain (different from Lenneberg's 'latent linguistic structure') which is activated when one makes an attempt to learn L_2.

To study interlanguage we have to study

(i) utterances produced by the learner in TL *i.e.*, IL utterances;

(ii) utterances produced in the NL of the learner by the learner;

(iii) utterances in the TL made by the native speaker.

Selinker argues that these are the only observable data that can be established for interlingual identification.

Selinker says that the most crucial fact that any description of interlanguage must account for is the phenomenon of fossilization He observes: "Fossilizable linguistic phenomena are linguistic items, rules and sub-systems which speakers of a particular NL will tend to keep in their interlanguage relative to a particular TL, no matter what the age of the learner or amount of explanation and instruction he receives in the TL." Selinker assumes that fossilization is another mechanism which exists in the latent psychological structure (*e.g.*, I want *that...* in Indian English).

The latent psychological structure, as discussed by Selinker, contains five central processes. These processes are:

(i) *Language Transfer* : Rules and sub-systems of the NL become part of the interlanguage. This process relates to interference.

(ii) *Transfer of Training* : The rules and sub-systems are a result of the identifiable items in training procedure *e.g.*, 'He' even when 'she' should be used.

(iii) *Strategies of L_2 learning* : The learner's approach to the material to be learned *e.g.*, the tendency on the part of the learner to reduce the TL to a simpler system. For instance, using all verbs in progressive.

(iv) *Strategies of L_2 communication* : The learner's approach to communication with speakers of the TL. A sub-conscious strategy of L_2 learning has been called 'cue-copying' *e.g.*, 'r' at the end of words like 'California' and 'saw' which foreign students of English who have had teachers from the Boston area regularly reproduce in their English IL.

(v) *Overgeneralization of the linguistic material* : Overgeneralization of the TL rules and semantic features *e.g.*, 'What did he intended to say' and 'drive a bicycle'.

Processes three, four and five relate to learning strategies. According to Selinker any one or more of these five processes could lead to fossilization of linguistic phenomena in the learner's interlanguage *i.e.*, certain erroneous forms will continue to occur in a learner's interlanguage relative to a particular TL even after a lot of exposure to it. It may be interesting to remember here that Indian English has been occasionally cited as a kind of interlanguage.

Jean D'Souza has suggested that Selinker's five processes may usefully be reduced to a threefold classification of the chief sources of error. The distinction Selinker draws between processes three, four, and five do not seem to D'Souza to be absolutely clear cut. D'Souza has suggested the following classification:

(a) transfer from previous language learning experience: errors due to interference

(b) Simplification and overgeneralization of elements of the target : language system

(c) errors arising from teaching methods and materials employed : teaching-induced errors.

Selinker has pointed out that beyond the five so-called central processes, there exist many other minor processes which account to some degree for the surface forms of Interlanguage utterances:

(i) Spelling pronunciation—'teacher'.

(ii) Cognate pronunciation—athlete as 'athit' by many Frenchmen.

(iii) holophrase learning—half-an-hour, so, 'one and half-an-hour'.

(iv) hypercorrection *e.g.*, the Israeli who in attempting to get rid of his uvular fricative for English retroflex [r] produces [w] before front vowels, 'a vocalization too far forward'.

The most significant point about interlanguage in relation to Contrastive Analysis and Error Analysis is the attitude towards the learner's performance, particularly towards the errors. Error analysts, by and large, consider errors to be harmful and attempt to do away with them. A student of interlanguage finds the deviations from the TL norm in interlanguage as exponents of the learner's system. Selinker speculates that as part of a definition of 'learning a second language', 'successful learning' of a second language for most learners, involves, to a large extent, *the reorganization of linguistic material* for an interlanguage to identify with a particular TL. Contrastive Analysis is mainly concerned with similarities with and differences, from NL. Significantly, interlanguage avoids this limitation. For Selinker, errors are a phenomenon of an *interlanguage*. As a result of the application of interlanguage studies to the foreign language teaching there would be a remarkable change in the attitude of the teachers towards the learner's performance. Selinker is fully convinced of the importance of learner language. The student of learner language may make a significant contribution to materials production. It is found that the learner goes ahead following 'an internal syllabus' of his own, then a better 'fit' could be discovered between the learner's learning syllabus and the teacher's teaching one.

It has been said that Interlanguage has implications for theories of language contact, language change and language acquisition and is also useful in describing special language types such as immigrant speech, non-standard dialect, non-native varieties of language and the language of aphasics and of poetry.

It should be noted, however, that if remedial materials are prepared sincerely, most errors can be got rid of. But an attempt to do too much at a time might cause serious difficulties and lead to frustration. The end-of-unit test should determine whether or not the learner should go ahead to the next unit. The end-of-programme test will help in deciding whether or not the learner continues the remedial programme. If the same errors are committed by many students they can be taken up at a group level and occasional and infrequent errors in small tutorial classes.

Let us now study specimen remedial measures with regard to prepositions, articles and spelling, appropriate to our requirements.

Preposition

The teacher can devise a number of excercises with a view to teaching preposition. It would be better to teach prepositions through situation, action chains, pictorial demonstration and story method. A picture can be hung on the wall and a passage given on the blackboard with blanks. The students can be asked to look at the picture and then to fill the gaps with certain prepositions, say at-in-on. The teacher can also construct a large number of substitution tables to teach these items: for example, the following to teach 'at' (in yes/no question form).

<table>
<tr><td rowspan="2">Were</td><td colspan="2">You</td><td rowspan="2">at</td><td rowspan="2">breakfast
lunch
dinner
tea
supper</td><td rowspan="2">yester-
day</td><td rowspan="2">?</td></tr>
<tr><td>the</td><td>man
women
players</td></tr>
</table>

The following tables provide more of a challenge because they force the learner *to think* about the sentences he is producing, as it is possible that he may come up with an incorrect or inappropriate sentence if he is not careful.

The	left stone motor-car stick pot match	is	in on near under	the	stone motor-car stick pot match chair

Your father Your brothers He	has have	known lived taught eaten	in Patna Russian sugar Mr. Sinha	since for	five years last November January

Puppet shows have also been recommended as useful audiovisual aids in the English class to teach prepositions. This can be done with the help of a story or a game. The prepositions of place (on, in, over, into, etc.) can be taught by using gestures and symbols.

It is advisable to make a logical gradation of preposition following the simple principles of *difficulty* and *frequency*. Less difficult uses, it should be remembered, are to be taught first and use in temporal circumstances should be taken up only after use in spatial circumstances has been done satisfactorily. The following exercise will make the student think of prepositions, among other things. Each sentence has been written with four endings of which one, or two may be correct. Write down the sentence number and the correct letter or letters only :

(i) We lent
- (a) Rs. 5 to Mohan.
- (b) to Mohan Rs. 5?
- (c) Mohan Rs. 5.
- (d) Rs. 5 Mohan.

(ii) Hand
- (a) me that book, please.
- (b) to me that book, please.
- (c) that book me, please.
- (d) that book to me, please.

(iii) Excuse
- (a) for coughing me.
- (b) me for coughing.

(c) for me coughing.
(d) coughing me.

(iv) We bought
(a) Rahim a horse.
(b) a horse for Rahim.
(c) for Rahim a horse.
(d) a horse Rahim.

The students can be asked to insert prepositions in the blanks: for example, in the following letter.

Ranchi,

Dear Mobi, 24th December, 1980.

Thanks very much—your letter. I received it last Monday. I am sorry I could not write—you. I have been very busy—my preparation —the ensuing examination. In addition—that my mother has not been well. Because of this I had a lot—extra things—do—home. My sister does the house work and the cooking, but I have—do the shopping. In fact I have just now come back—the market.

I am sorry that I can't write you a longer letter. I will try—write more next time.

With best wishes,

Yours sincerely,
Azfar

Interesting multiple-choice type exercises can be set. The following is an example.

Complete each sentence correctly with one of the four words underneath it. Only one of the words is correct :

(1) Supermarkets deal — nearly every kind of foodstuff.

on, at, with, in

(2) She agreed — her mother about the holiday plan.

with, to, over, for

(3) The firm supplied him — a car.

for, with, by, of

(4) Shortage of money added — her problems.

on, at, with, to

(5) They insisted — taking the exam. too soon.

on, for, to, in

(6) We congratulated Dilip — winning the award.
for, by, on, at

(7) They depend — their mother for money.
to, at, with, on

(8) My uncle borrowed Rs. 100—my father.
of, at, from, to

(9) The Mugal ruled — a very large kingdom.
on, over, for, towards

(10) She was accused — taking a tin of cheese.
of, for, at, by

(11) They quarrelled — the choice of a house.
on for, over, to

(12) Next week you must enrol—the new term.
at, to, in, for

Articles

It will be very helpful if the classroom teacher is aware of the L_1 of his students. Even if he is not the native speaker of the language he can learn from his friends and colleagues the important points in the use of the article so that when he teaches in the classroom he should be aware of the interference caused by the L_1 in this area. The teacher should make it a point to spend sufficient time and energy on teaching the articles (and also reteaching, if necessary). He can prepare a number of remedial exercises or borrow them from standard books and recent research works. Carefully prepared exercises and substitution tables can lead to a better understanding of the grammatical item. Needless to say, the students should realize that the omission or insertion of these articles is often meaningful and significant. Through use of these articles in different contexts, the classroom teacher can make them understand this. The following substitution tables can be cited as examples:

<table>
<tr><td rowspan="3">That's</td><td>a</td><td>useful
useless</td><td></td><td rowspan="2">book</td></tr>
<tr><td>an</td><td>ugly</td><td></td></tr>
<tr><td>a university</td><td colspan="3">an umbrella</td></tr>
</table>

<table>
<tr><td rowspan="2">Can</td><td rowspan="2">You
John
Mary</td><td rowspan="2">play</td><td>the</td><td>trumpet
violin
piano</td><td>?</td></tr>
<tr><td colspan="2">tennis
football
cricket</td><td>?</td></tr>
</table>

A picture can be placed before the students who can be asked to describe the same. The teacher has to moderate this venture and see that definite and indefinite articles are properly used.

Suitable exercises can be constructed to teach articles; for example—

Rewrite the following sentences after making the necessary corrections :

They went for a picnic on the Sunday.

The Shakespeare was a great dramatist.

We shall reach the Poona in the morning.

Suresh took his examination in the April.

Use 'a', 'an' or 'the' to fill the blank spaces below (where necessary):

Hasan was—clever man. He lived in—city of Baghdad.— people of Baghdad said he was—cleverest man in—whole of—Iraq. Hasan had—neighbour who was—rich merchant, but—great miser.

One day—merchant heard Hasan—praying to—God. He was asking—God for—lot of money. He said he wanted 9,999 dinars, and would return—money if—God sent him—dinar more or less.

—merchant put 10,000 dinars in—bag and threw—bag into—Nasiruddin's house. He wanted to see if his neighbour was really —honest man.

Spelling

In general, the Incidental method and the Drill method are employed in the teaching of English spelling. In the incidental method, spelling is taught only incidentally and casually. The following kinds of drills may be used in the Drill method:

(i) The Oral Drill

(ii) The Motor Drill

(iii) The Visual Drill.

Spelling drill with particular stress on the part of the world found difficult by the pupils will be of special help to them. Why not give them phonetic symbols, say the symbols used by Hornby and others in the ALD of Current English? Let us tell them how and when to use this dictionary for both meaning and pronunciation purposes.

On the basis of the performance of his students a teacher with considerable experience can easily draft a list of words which his pupils are likely to misspell. He should arrange a weekly test of ten or more words. At the end of ten weeks or so the students should be tested on all the words listed. Undoubtedly, this will make them alert and thus cautious regarding spelling. The students must be told clearly that a large number of errors of spelling in their writings is a definite sign of lack of education and respectability.

It would be helpful if words similar in pronunciation and almost similar in spelling were grouped under separate heads *e.g.*, the following groups :

(i) Words of common auditory elements—pail, pale, not, nought, there, their.

(ii) Words of similar visual but dissimilar auditory elements *e.g.*, stove, glove, strove etc.

(iii) Words with silent letters *e.g.*, doubt, debt, drought.

The students should be asked to correct wrong spellings. Exercises like 'Supply the missing vowels' etc. can be constructed. 'Spot' dictations have been suggested to test the spelling of words in contexts. A number of mnemonics can also be used for this purpose, *e.g.*,

Acknowledge — There is an *edge* in acknowledge.
Arrangement — There is a *gem* in arrangement.
Amateur — Remember *ate* in amateur.
Attendance — *At ten* (we will) *dance*.
Innocent — *In no cent* is there much buying power.
Conscience — *Con* plus *science* equals conscience.
Villain — The villain enjoyed his *villa in* the hills.
Benefited — He is a *fit* person to be benefited.

With the help of pieces of chalk of different colours we can teach the spelling of the problem words on the blackboard *e.g.*,

— Let the difficult part stand out : Underline the difficulty;
— Cal en *dar* or circle the key part : Calen (dar)
— misspelling : do'nt miss the miss here
— achievement : look for *eve* in achievement and believe
— When you *ascertain* you become *as certain* as possible
— to get her — is to be *together*

Exercises like the following can also be constructed.

(1) Select the correct word:

(i) The sudden smoke (blured, blurred) his vision.
(ii) She (stared, starred) as the heroine of the film.
(iii) The low-calorie diet should make you (slimer, slimmer).
(iv) The (robber, rober) made away with the crown jewels.

(2) (i) Give another word like *mouse* which ends in-*ouse*, and use this word in a sentence.

(ii) Make as many words as you can which end in-*aw*, like *paw*, and use this word in a sentence.

(iii) Give six words which begin with *re*, like *repay*, and use each word in a sentence.

(iv) Give a word which rhymes with *doubt* and then say which letter in *doubt* is not sounded.

(v) Make new words by adding *-ing* to each of these words; begin, lie, try, sit, have, roll and run.

(vi) Make other words by placing another letter in front of the following—he, am, or, an, out.

(vii) Make new words by placing another letter at the end of each of the following—of, me, no, on, in.

(viii) The word *night* rhymes with *kite*. Give some other words which end in-*ight* and have the same sound. Use each word in a sentence.

(ix) Give words which rhyme with *eyes* and use each in a sentence.

(x) Make any new words you can from the letters in the word *especially*.

The teacher can write on the blackboard several words with their letters jumbled. Two teams are formed and the pupils from the two teams alternatively take a word and give its correct spelling. The teacher can give a crossword puzzle and the team that solves first wins. These should not contain rare and archaic words. Flash cards can also be used as an aid. Spelling games provide interest and stimulate learning (*e.g.*, word building, spelling bee, completion game, and memory game), Mackey (1965) has mentioned the magician's game in which the learner is given the problem of changing one word into another by changing only one letter at a time. Each change must itself be a word. For example, the teacher can ask the students to change *dog* into *cat*;

Dog			Cat
dog	dot	cot	cat

The effectiveness of instructional procedures in this area is largely dependent on the development of proper attitudes. These attitudes can be stimulated by showing the students that the words taught are the ones they are most likely to need now and in the future. Encouraging in the class a spirit of natural pride and cooperation in spelling achievement should also be rewarding.

REFERENCES

Bhatia, Aban T. 1975. "Error Analysis and its Implications for Language Teaching", *IJOAL*, Vol. 1, Number 2.

Burt, M.K. and Kiparsky C. 1972. The *Gooficon.* Newburry House, Rowley, Massachusett.

Candler, W.J. 1979. "Errors, and, Text in Multidialect Setting", *ELT* Journal, Vol. XXXIII, Number 4.

Close, R.A. 1972. *English as a Foreign Language*, London (1972).

Djordjevic, R. 1976. "Comparing L_1 and L_2 : Implications for Teaching", *IJOAL*, Vol. II, No. 1.

D'Souza, Jean, 1979. "Error Analysis—A Survey of Presant Views", *CIEFL* Newsletter, Vol. XIII, No. 3 & 4.

French, F.G. 1949. *Common Errors in English*, London : OUP (1963 impression consulted).

Galarcep, Marietta Fernandez, "Puppets in Teaching English Language", *ELT* Journal, Vol. XX, No. 3.

Lee, W.R. "The Linguistic Context of Language Teaching", In : *Teaching English as a Second Language*, 1865 Edit, H.B. Allen.

Mackey, W.F., 1965. *Language Teaching Analysis*, London : Longman.

Morgan, D.Y., "A Discussion of Remedial Teaching", In : *ELT Selections* 2, 1967. Edit. W.R. Lee, OUP.

Nöth, Winfred, 1979. "Errors as a Discovery Procedure in Linguistics", *IRAL,* XVII/1.

Parashar, S.V. 1977-78. "Current Trends in Error Analysis", JSL, Vol. V, Number 1 and 2.

Pit Corder, S. 1973. *Introducing Applies Linguistics*, Penguin.

Pittman, G.A. 1967. *Teaching Structural English*, Ginn & Co. Ltd.

Richards, Jack C. 1974 (edit), *Error Analysis*, Longman.

Sharma, S.K. 1980. "Practical and Theoretical Consideration included in Error Analysis," *IJOAL*, Vol. VI, No. 2.

Sridhar, S.N., "Contrastive Analysis, Error Analysis and Interlanguage: Three Phases of one Goal", *Indian Linguistics*, Vol. 37, Number 4.

Verma, S.K. 1974. *Linguistics : Introductions to English Language Teaching,* Vol. I, Delhi : OUP.

9

LINGUISTICS AND LANGUAGE TEACHING

"It is probably fair to say", Paul Roberts said in 1960, "that Linguistics is the hottest topic on the English teachers' agenda at the present time." In fact, Linguistics is even now "almost certain to be on the programme whenever English teachers come together." The study of Linguistics has acquired popularity and respectability basically because language interests us and the problems posed by language are intellectual challanges. Some people, however, demand that a science should prove its usefulness though it is generally considered pointless to put the question, "Why pursue knowledge?" Linguistics is just a baby science but, with the passage of time, it has already started finding applications in so many fields. Till the other day the common opinion was that Linguistics had no application: the subject was thought of as knowledge for its own sake and as having no direct utility. The continued work in the field and allied fields have brought to the fore the applied side of the subject so as to make even the worst critics of Linguistics on this score realize its significance. Now Linguistics has turned out to have many specific and practical applications. The knowledge of the subject has been useful in various areas.

It is important to remember here that in the present context a great contribution of Linguistics is to help us realize that each dialect or language is rich enough to serve the requirements of its speakers. We must cultivate tolerance towards other dialects and languages. Prof. Healey of the University of Surrey forecasts that changing attitude and new educational techniques are producing a new generation of multilinguals capable of breaking down long-standing language barriers. Staffordshire constabulary have taken to learning different languages in a big way because they hope it will help them in controlling traffic. It should be noted here that policemen in Lancashire have been learning Urdu and Gujrati and servicemen preparing for posting abroad or training as interpreters attend courses of varying lengths in a number of languages. To equip them for interpreter duties, Royal Air Force linguists spend 15 hours a day working on high-powered year-long Russian and Chinese language courses. This has led one United States Air Force Colonel to describe the British forces as "possibly the most efficient language teachers in the world". It should be added here, however, that in the Unites States, too, a widespread application of structural linguistics was made to teach a foreign language to soldiers during the Second World War and the approach was called Army Specialized Training Programme (ASTP). It provided intensive courses in various languages with special emphasis on speaking and understanding the spoken form. The method succeeded with the American army as motivation to learn the language was very high. As it was difficult to generate a similar type of motivation amongst the normal learners of a foreign language, the method slowly and steadily fell into disuse after the Second World War.

By Applied Linguistics many people mean General Linguistics in its application to language teaching though now Applied Linguistics is the name given to the applications of the subject to the activities serving certain aims (Applied Linguistics is the application of Linguistics to language use, including teaching—Widdowson, 1980). One of the reasons for the sudden birth of an applied linguistics during, and shortly after World War II was "the new situation created by war and post-war conditions: the need for rapid instruction in numerous unknown languages which,... became a necessity in almost all parts of the world where liberation, occupation and administration of foreign territories created a need for practical acquaintance with foreign languages" (Malmberg, 1971). In June 1969 issue of *The Linguistic Reporter* W.R. O'Donnel described an applied linguist as a person who concerns himself with practical language problems and brings to bear on them those aspects of Linguistics and allied fields which will contribute toward their solution. While this view may not be acceptable to all linguists, particularly those who apply themselves to highly theoretical considerations, it should be acknowledged that the practical application of Linguistics is important in its own right. By the same token, "it should be acknowledged by the practising teacher ... that the application of linguistic concepts and tools to practical language problems requires much more than a passing acquaintance with linguistic theory" (Strain, 1971). Ferguson divides Applied Linguistics into various common branches : the creation and revision of writing systems, literacy efforts, translation work, language teaching efforts, and language policy efforts.

The field of language teaching has much bigger public. In fact, Linguistics has a contribution to make in any situation in which language is being taught because it makes better descriptions of language (both native and foreign). Providing good descriptions based on sound linguistic principles is perhaps the main contribution that the linguistic sciences can make to the teaching of languages. In fact, the claim that any description of language implies Linguistics is not unfair. Linguistics discovers more and more about the way language functions. Pit Corder (1973) argues that the description of language is itself the first stage in the application of linguistic theory with reference to teaching, in that it defines what the nature of the language to be taught is; subsequent stages in the application of linguistics to language teaching consider what is to be taught and how it is to be organised and presented. Talking of instruction in the native language, Marckwardt (1970) has remarked that "it is in the expansion as well as the fixation of language patterns that linguistic knowledge may be put to advantageous use, both in warning the student of the pitfalls involved in inadequately controlled expression and in making him aware of the resources of the language." He is of the view that the knowledge of language which Linguistics provides can help the teachers in coping with many of the language problems that arise. He is not off the mark when he says that Linguistics will not furnish the sole answer, but it can be a significant help in many instances if the teacher is equipped to make an intelligent and sophisticated use of it." To quote Sumner Ives : "I should confess, nay insist, that linguistics simply gives the teacher additional or more effective tools and a better understanding of what he is working with. Any improvement he makes in his knowledge of language, any details he learns about the actual forms and constructions of English, will make him a more expert instructor."

Another domain in which this knowledge has been made use of is translation. Our understanding of the universals of language and semantics can help us handle the problems of translation effectively. Translation implies transference of meaning which can hardly be effected without a reasonably sophisticated knowledge of the language concerned on the part of the translator. Linguistics has a definite role in the training of translators and interpreters.

In machine translation, precise specifications of procedures and the materials the machine will follow are necessary. Machine translation will be honest and crude and, therefore, editing will be essential. All this often involves higher cost than human translation. If the grammars of the two languages are stored in the computer and the links provided between them, the computer will start with one language and translate sentences into the other. The analysis of one language should match with the analysis of the other for which a kind of transfer grammar will be helpful. The conventional expressions and expressions used as phatic communion are best translated by the equivalent conventions in the other language, substituted mechanically and not by looking at the meanings of the constituents. A word-for-word approach is largely inadequate. The translation of trick sentences or ambiguous sentences often creates problems and one faces difficulty in the treatment of "discontinuity" as well. The translation of longer sentences is far more complex. Many people think that machine translation will make the mastery of more than one language unnecessary. This does not appear to be a realistic assessment. Anyone who wishes to communicate quickly will have to speak several languages. The use of computer has, however, begun to spread into language teaching. Much interest has developed in recent years in the fields of individualization, distance learning and computer assisted learning. Considering the cost, effort and other problems a large scale adoption of computer-assisted language teaching programmes does not appear very likely, at least in the near future. Hays (1971) lists the main purposes for which computational linguistics has been applied: "Translation from one language to another; topical analysis to determine the subject-matter of a text in systems for information storage and retrieval; attitudinal analysis to determine the feelings and purposes of the author in social-science content analysis; narrative analysis, as in studies of folklore; and stylistic analysis, as in the study of literature".

A good knowledge of Linguistics is necessary in dialect survey and dialect geography. Geographical Linguistics presents a vivid picture of the social forces which lie behind linguistic change. Dialect maps and dialect atlas have been found very helpful. The knowledge of Linguistics has been fruitfully utilized in such fields as Communication Engineering, Script Reform and Lexicography (the writing and compiling of dictionaries—monolingual, bilingual and trilingual). The dictionaries should keep "abreast of the theories and researches in linguistics" (Warfel, 1961). Roman Jakobson and other linguists provided a framework that was of help to communication engineers in the study of the acoustic signal. Linguistics plays a role of considerable importance in spelling modernization and reducing sounds to a system of writing. As for the adult literacy programmes, the linguist has an important role to play in the selection and organisation of the teaching material and he must work out the principles which are congenial and natural to the particular languages in lexical creation such as root derivation, compounding and borrowing (Annamalai, 1975). Experienced linguists should be associated if the languages of the developing nations are to be codified. The linguist has to be consulted in the matters of linguistic policy (Malmberg, 1971).

The Olinguistics, Sociolinguistics, Anthroplogical Linguistics, Mathematical Linguistics, Psycholinguistics and Neurolinguistics are some other interesting and useful branches of the subject. Mathematical Linguistics tries to answer certain questions *e.g.*, what words are to be considered of high frequency and hence to be included in a minimum vocabulary and which must be discarded? Anthropologists have used "culture to understand language. It is all a bit circular; nevertheless, the anthroplogical view of language and culture has provided some important insights and implications for language teaching in general and teaching English as a second language in particular" (Siegel, 1980). The idea of combining linguistic facts with cultural content has been gaining support among leading methodologists (Verescagin and Kostomorov, 1981).

Of late, there has been an increasing awareness of the importance of understanding the cognitive process in facilitating language learning. It was realized that repeated pattern drills or routine remedial exercises did not necessarily enhance language proficiency. Aptitude, motivation and such other extra-curricular but equally important parameters influence the process of language learning. It was felt that the insights from psychology regarding the process of brain functioning should also be incorporated in planning English language teaching programmes. The direct influence of all this has been psycholinguistics, a branch which deals exclusively with the influence of the mind on teaching/learning. "Lately, psycholinguistics has come to he recognised as a discipline in its own rights as a system to investigate the implications of linguistics to the psychological processes, both normal and abnormal" (Verma, 1982). While addressing the Summer School in Psychology, Pattanayak (1971) said: "A host of theoretical and experimental approaches in disciplines like linguistics, psychology and communication engineering concerning what Sebeok and Osgood call 'the relationship between messages and the characteristics of human individuals who select and interpret them' has resulted in a field of study which may be called psycholinguistics. It is not a new science, a new discipline independent of psychology and linguistics, but an inter-disciplinary approach to building up a common framework of a theoretical model applicable to differing kinds of data and differing approaches to these data concerning the characteristics of messages, their use, their manipulation and interpretation."

Neurolinguistics represents a synthesis of brain sciences, the behavioural sciences and the clinical sciences, regardless of whether one's primary interest is in language, in the brain, or in the rehabilitation of the brain-damaged individual. The term neurolinguistics began to be used after 1962 in connection with speech pathology. Neurolinguistics has been defined (Hcaen and Dubois, 1971) as the application of the methods and models of linguistics to the study of disturbances of the realization of speech caused by cortical lesions. Grewel (1966) defined it as the study of language and speech disorders due to neurolingual impairment. Luria (1967) states that neurolinguistics should transcend the mere clinical description of language disorders—it should set up models that help uncover the neuro-psychological basis of language impairment.

Linguistic knowledge has been utilized in speech therapy for patients whose speech mechanisms have been damaged or are imperfect as a defect or as a result of injury. If the child trips up on s, sch, ch and j sounds probably it is the teeth that are at fault. A common palate defect like cleft palate may cause poor articulation of consonant sounds like k, kh, g, gh, t, d and z. It may make the voice nasal and hence unintelligible. If the child's trouble is with articulation, the therapist may prescribe certain tongue exercises to maintain mouth pressure to pronounce certain sounds like p, b, m, n, s, ch and chh which require the sudden release of breath. Often correct breathing patterns have to be established and ear training has to be given to distinguish between a correct and a faulty voice. Without good insight into linguistic functions, which is the linguist's (phonetician's) competence, no successful treatment of language and speech disorders is possible. Phonetics plays an important part in the field of deaf teaching and deaf education. In fact, the famous teachers of the deaf of the sixteenth and seventeenth centuries founded articulatory phonetics (Malmberg, 1969). The therapist needs to know the amount of linguistic information to give the child in his own utterances and the level of utterances to demand back from him. It is believed that a rationale for treatment can be based upon linguistic factors. A child's degree of experimentation can be revealed by linguistic analysis and this will enable the therapist to provide the information the child needs to complete his system (Brown, 1969).

Though in the realm of language teaching the importance of Linguistics cannot be overemphasized the question often raised is what quantum of it the language teachers actually need. It may be noted here that language teaching has a number of dimensions *i.e.*, description of the native language and the target language, comparison of NL with TL (Contrastive Linguistics) and selecting, grading, presenting and testing items. It has been stressed by Lado and many others that Contrastive Linguistics has an illuminating explanatory power and is of special interest to the language teacher because in its terms items can be graded. Contrastive Analysis presents a descriptive study of two or more languages. The descriptions can be made at various levels—lexical, grammatical, semantic and phonological. The differences are often the chief sources of difficulty in learning a second language. It is expected that by looking at the similarities and differences we will succeed as teachers to locate the areas particularly found difficult by our students in learning the target language. The linguist takes up each phoneme in the native language and compares it with the phonetically most similar one in the second language. He takes up the sequences of phonemes and does likewise. Morphemes and syntax patterns are also compared and the differences described. "Contrastive Linguistics ... for the most part compares languages with the quite utilitarian aim of improving the methods and results of language teaching" (Nickel, 1971). Often when the student is uncertain about the correct mode of expressing his ideas in the foreign language, he reverts to the pattern of his own (Grauberg, 1969). The results of these contrastive descriptions form the basis for the preparation of instructional materials, texts and tests. However, it should be borne in mind that there are a number of limitations of Contrastive Linguistics *e.g.*, it cannot predict all the areas likely to be found difficult by learners and some of its predictions may not prove true at all.

Stylistics and Error Analysis are being widely used these days and for them also a background in Linguistics is necessary. An increasing number of teachers of literature seem to be finding that valuable supplementary insights are obtainable through various linguistic approaches. Linguistic literary stylistics is constantly using the ongoing developments of linguistics to open up new avenues of stylistic approach and analysis. "Stylistics being a theory of literature as well as a methodology of literary study, furnishes, on the one hand, certain frame of reference to the goal of teaching poetry and, on the other hand, provides certain conditions for carrying on this goal" (Srivastava, 1985). Error Analysis enables the teachers to go to the level of the students themselves and to have a look at their difficulties and to find out the areas where they need special help. The classification of different types of errors and the establishment of their relative frequencies will be, to a large extent, futile exercises unless at the same time we are trying to find out why errors are made. Recognition description and explanation are the three usual stages. The explanation of errors can be regarded as a linguistic problem *i.e.,* a statement of the way the learner has deviated from the realization rules of the target language in the derivation of his sentence, that is, what rules he has violated, substituted or disregarded. The successive linguistic systems *i.e.*, the analysis of the intermediate stages that a learner constructs on his way from a zero language state to the proficiency in a target language has been called Interlanguage by Selinker. 'Interlanguage' can be used in order to gauge the abilities of the learner in the process of learning.

It may not be out of place to mention here that language teaching has different aspects : the organisational, the technological, the psychological (language acquisition, memory, motivation etc.), the sociological (attitude to language, use of language,

language in society etc.), the pedagogical (selecting, grading, presenting and testing) and the linguistic (scientific description and comparison). The organisation of second language teaching gives rise to a number of problems. It goes without saying that no teacher teaches the entire language at once. He selects, stages and grades his materials. Grading, as we know, is a complex process of grouping and sequencing interrelated patterns in terms of increasing complexity. Linguistics comes in here and offers linguistically graded phonological, syntactic and lexical patterns. Linguistic insight can be profitably used to group related patterns and formulate productive rules. Once selection and gradation are accomplished Linguistics comes in good measure. Lennon (1988) charges that the influence of Linguistics on language teaching has been largely concentrated on syllabus and materials design rather than on educational policy or classroom teaching. Lennon (1988) observes : "Ideas do not flow from linguistics to teaching via the critical and testing medium of applied linguistics."

Interesting experiments have been made in the field of language teaching on the basis of linguistic theories. Stern (1983) points out : "No language teacher—however strenuously he may deny his interest in theory—can teach a language without a theory of language teaching, even if it is only implicit in value judgments, decisions and actions, or in the organizational pattern within which he operates." Stern refers to this theory, which the teacher is unconscious of, as an "implicit" theory. However, if the teacher does not advance from this "implicit" theory to more conscious assumptions, principles and concepts underlying (his) actions "then his theory is a 'weak' one. Further without explicitness no critical discussion, hence no advance in thought would be possible" (Stern, 1983). Barnes has shown teachers the way to extract theory out of their own classroom talk by making tapescripts of their lessons and analysing the various kinds of questions asked. He argues that a large part of the curriculum, called Methodology exists in a hidden form in Teacher-Pupil talk.

Chomsky's pronouncements played an important role in this area during the fifties and thereafter. Noam Chomsky thought that the brain was a kind of magic box where with limited inputs unlimited outputs could be obtained. The brain is able to generate an infinite number of sentences though only a finite number of them have been learnt or taught. The theory of Chomsky went directly against the basis of structural linguistics. Language learning, according to structuralists, was a process of habit formation and all that the teachers were supposed to do was to train a learner to react in a particular language situation. During the fifties, the teachers largely rejected the structural approach and began to pay more attention to the psychologists for evolving methods and materials for language teaching. At this time, they started emphasizing the significance of theories (*e.g.*, the theories of 'perception', 'acquisition', 'behaviour' etc.) with regard to language teaching. The twentieth century linguistics has contributed so much to teaching methods and technique because structural linguistics took up two aspects of fundamental interest for all sorts of pedagogical applications : language as a structure and language as a social phenomenon. At times, as Malmberg (1969) remarks, "The tendency to switch over from classical structuralism to generative and transformational grammar has been followed by a corresponding modification of teaching methods."

The non-structural approaches are chiefly based on communicative and cognitive theories. They attempt to demolish the entire edifice of structural teaching. These theories led to an awareness that the process of learning in a human brain goes on in a manner often difficult to explain. The complexity of this process of language learning has convinced the experts in the field of language teaching that human beings need not be forced to go through intensive practice drills to behave in a language situation. On the other hand, inputs can be so arranged that sufficient amount of language learning takes place. The theories of knowledge, capacity and competence and the like have also been studied and developed and applied to the English language teaching (or foreign language teaching). Skinner's theory of 'operant conditioning' of behaviour and the linear programme of self-instruction in language teaching have been perhaps notable examples of this kind of application in so far as language teaching is concerned. "Whereas the audiolingual method was exclusively based on Skinnerian operant conditioning, and the neo-cognitive method as espoused by Carroll (1966) and the cognitive anti-method (Newmark 1979) were strongly derivative of Chomskyan linguistic ideas, materials such as Johnson's *Communicate in Writing* (1979) or White's *Functional English* (1979) are eclectic. Their central informing principle is that of functionalism/communicativeness, which can be traced back to Austin (1962), Searle (1969), Campbell and Wales (1970), and Hymes (1971), but they draw on a wide variety of linguistic theories" (Lennon, 1988). A clear example of eclecticism is *A Grammar of Contemporary English* (Quirk et al 1972). Some new methods have developed in recent years. Krashen's Input Method and Asher's Total Physical Response Method (Krashen 1982; Asher 1969) are only weakly based on Chomskyan linguistics and language-acquisition research. Essentially, they are the result of classroom experimentation in the light of current ideas, rather than the implementation of a whole linguistic theory. They are essentially empirical and pragmatic (Lennon, 1988). Other methods of this nature are Terrel's Natural approach and Lazanov's Suuggestopedia. The fact remains that the knowledge of linguistics will be helpful not only in the selection of a particular method or methods suitable for particular language teaching situations but also in devising one's own method or an eclectic approach. Linguistics for language teaching should describe the nature of language as a communicative system as also its varieties as used in a wide range of contexts.

Great changes have taken place in the field of language teaching and the extent of the change has been so vast of late that it has been referred to as a revolution. Strevens has made an interesting comparison: he compares the change in language teaching with the application of scientific knowledge and techniques to the change as a result of the conversion of the textile industry from a *craft* to an *applied science*. Language laboratories have been set up. Objective testing to assess progress, specialized materials, intensive teaching and programmed instruction are some interesting and useful things in use these days. In fact, the entire perspective has changed and language is no longer taken as a set of facts to be crammed : it is now considered as a patterned social behaviour. This view of language makes it imperative that one should teach lists of words through structures in which utterances containing those words are proper *e.g.*, "This is a book" and "Ram is not present in the class today."

In the new approach grammar does not always get the upper hand. Damien Sherlock, the then General Manager of the Berlitz Schools in Britain, once said : "You don't have to be a mechanic to drive a car. It is the same with foreign languages—you don't have to master every minute detail of grammar to communicate." In these schools teachers and pupils speak the language under instruction.

The aim of the new approach is to make the learner 'experience' language in a situation that is as nearly real as possible. Mention may be made here of the situational method, notional syllabuses and the various projects for telephone, radio and television teaching. The magic of electronics is rapidly providing more advanced machinery for the teaching of languages. While suggesting a set of model classroom activities to facilitate the learning of English, McLean (1980) remarks that 'experience' should come before interpretation—"Before the students find the rules of the language it is essential that they are given enough exposure, so that they can experience the language before learning the rules governing it." To avoid being outdated the latest recordings and texts should be used. These exciting methods motivate the students making teaching interesting.

Jack Stein once referred to language teaching as the amateur profession. Moulton (1970) feels that language teaching is bound and doomed to remain an amateur profession just as long as it lacks a comprehensive theory on which to base its daily teaching practice. It should be mentioned here, in passing, that the linguistic materials meant for teachers are generally presented in a form and in a language quite specialized and remote from that of the educated laymen. As more and more teachers should try to understand the scientific work in Linguistics it is necessary that more books bearing in mind these requirements should be published by linguists incorporating the latest developments. The writers of these books should try to be more widely understood.

It is said that the teaching of foreign languages is now one of the world's major occupations and teaching a foreign or a second language, in particular, has been considered a linguistic task. Therefore, big leaps have been made in this area. It should be stressed here that if our understanding of language in general improves we will be able to perform the task of teaching languages in a much better manner and, consequently, our performance will improve in all aspects *e.g.*, techniques of teaching and production of textbooks. Many think that Linguistics can go a long way in helping classroom teachers reshape their view of language and language teaching. It is reasonable to expect that a teacher who has some insight into the mechanism of language can face the problems of language teaching with greater confidence and efficiency.

An important aim of the second language teaching is that we prepare the learner to perform a specific set of roles in a new language and new culture. In this domain, again, Linguistics can offer some guidelines in terms of registral analysis of language varieties and socio-economic patterning. It may be added here that register-shift *i.e.*, the ability to shift registers according to shifts in the situation, is one of the significant conditions for success in handling a second language effectively. A teacher should understand the particular language situations properly. One can easily see the widespread application of new methods and techniques in English language teaching where new market sectors have grown up, most noticeably in ESP and EAP (Lennon, 1988).

It is interesting to note that some people claim that Linguistics is not at all essential to language teaching, that without the study of Linguistics the progress of the work is not likely to hamper much and that the best course is to free language teachers from the trammels of linguistic theory. It is said that teachers and pupils absolutely untrained in Linguistics are all the time teaching and learning. There is no doubt that we cannot say that Linguistics can generate ready answers to all the questions which have been worrying the language, teachers for ages.

Wilkins's remarks are worth quoting here : "It would be absurd to pretend that no one can be a good teacher unless he has a knowledge of Linguistics" — "It would be equally foolish to derive one's approach to language teaching solely from Linguistics and Psychology." Halliday et al observe : "Whatever the place of Phonetics and Linguistics may be in language teaching, the formulation of linguistic statements is by no means essential to language learning." Chomsky finds it "difficult to believe that either Linguistics or Psychology has achieved a theoretical understanding that might enable it to support a technology of language teaching". Lennon (1988), too, charges that Linguistics has, in many ways, failed to offer the language teacher a description of the language to be taught, information as to teaching content, organisation and presentation as envisaged by Corder (1973) and that, years after Wilkins (1972), language teaching is still at the mercy of fashion. It may be pointed out here that these are extreme views and, in fact, Wilkins has himself remarked elsewhere that Linguistics has done a commendable service to the language teacher in providing description, in determining the content of learning, in increasing the teacher's understanding of the essential nature of language. Wilkins cites three aims of Linguistics:

1. to study the human language faculty.
2. to develop theories to explain language behaviour.
3. to provide the most efficient means for describing languages and to make the most accurate and comprehensive descriptions available.

Lennon (1988) is of the opinion that "this definition makes provision not only for the descriptive concerns associated with the structural linguists, but also for the concerns of psycholinguistics, sociolinguistics, and the post-Chomskyan interest in language acquisition."

Linguistics certainly does not tell the teacher what to teach and how to teach and it does not offer any new technique of language teaching but, as a matter of fact, Linguistics makes him a better teacher by providing him insights into the language and deepening his understanding of it. Significantly the insights provided by Linguistics are helpful to the language teacher in all the four areas of Methodology—limitation, grading, presentation and testing. It has been rightly said, however, that Linguistics is not Methodology. There is hardly anything like a linguistic way of presenting material in the classroom. The study of Linguistics, however, enhances convenience, economy and speed. It presents a new orientation towards language and also a new way of determining the basic facts and features on which the students base their learning. Unquestionably, the old methods and materials also work but perhaps not well enough. The old methods are "still widely used throughout the world and appear to be quite unaffected by anything in applied linguistics or theoretical linguistics" (Lennon, 1988). They are, however, as has been aptly argued by some linguists, like candles which work even now but we use electric light.

The organisation and order in which the items should be presented in describing the language can be achieved systematically by a process that is itself chiefly linguistic. The organisation of items into a teachable pattern is generally called methodology. Linguistics provides principles with regard to moderating the practical procedures of teaching method. In the United States a great deal of attention is being paid to the linguistic side of the teaching job. A large number of classroom teachers in the United States are highly trained in Linguistics. On the other hand, methodology reigns supreme in the British approach. Those who prepare syllabuses, textbooks, tests and other tools of the language teaching profession and also those who train teachers must know their stuff in Linguistics and Phonetics. Linguistics, therefore, appears to be relevant to the requirements of the framer, the trainer and the teacher. It may be a safe minimum to conclude that the teacher should be aware of the existence of scientific linguistics. In fact, the process of teaching somebody with a view to enable him to use a language requires an intelligent use of both Linguistics and Methodology—a combination of both American and British approaches. Striking a balance between the two approaches is expected to be profitable. Linguistics carries more weight with the framers and trainers. Methodology, however, gets the upper hand in the classroom. "If teaching is defined as what goes on in the classroom, it is likely that in many classrooms the influence of such theoretical developments in linguistics as transformational generative grammar, speech acts, communicative competence, rules of grammar, and rules of use has been minimal" (Lennon, 1988). Lennon (1988) asserts that the competence of teachers rather than of the method remains more important.

What we need today, as Verma (1975) has said, is a healthy partnership between Linguistics and Methodology and a closer collaboration between linguists and language teachers. Lennon (1988) does not appear wholly impartial when he remarks that if "linguistics has, in many ways, failed language teachers, language teachers for their part have a wealth of information that has not been exploited by linguists"—"Perhaps linguistics has first to learn from language teachers and learners as a prelude to ultimately informing language teachers and language teaching". At the same time, it has been argued by some people, and not very unjustifiably, that Linguistics has not been very successful in language teaching chiefly because of the kind of Linguistics that is applied (*i.e.*, formal grammar). Linguistics, however, can give the language teachers, course designers and producers of materials an inside view of the organisation of language. What it should get in return is feedback on classroom tryouts. We are in a way faced with the well-known problem of the 'thinkers' being separated from the 'doers', the theorists *vs.* the practitioners. Needless to add, there should be a constant mutual feedback between theory and application. Chomsky feels that "teachers in particular have a responsibility to make sure (the linguist's) ideas and proposals are evaluated on their merits and not passively accepted .... It is the language teacher himself who must validate or refute any specific proposal." In fact, the English language teaching community should be allowed to get actively involved in generating a pedagogy which combines the findings of research and of the new approaches with teachers' own pedagogical instincts. The uncritical and unthinking applications of theories to language teaching have been sometimes unhappy experiences. Krashen (1982) talks of behaviourism which, in the specific form of Skinnerian operant conditioning, was taken over into Linguistics and then applied to language teaching. According to Lennon (1988), "Unthinking attempts to apply transformational grammar to language teaching are equally infelicitous...in that the theory describes native speaker competence rather than the process by which a learner may achieve competence in a second language."

Perhaps it would be appropriate to conclude with this remark of Hill: "It is the linguists who need linguistics.....It is we who have the task of making linguistics sufficiently adult, and its results sufficiently available so that all people of good will, who work within the field of language, language art, and language usage can realize that there are techniques and results which are of value to them."

REFERENCES

Annamalai, E. (1975). The Role of Linguistics in adult literacy programmes. *Indian Linguistics*. Vol. 36. No. 3.

Barnes, Douglas (1975). *From Communication to Curriculam*. Penguin.

Brown, B.B. (1971). A. Suggested Rationale for the Treatment of Developmental Disorders of Language. In : *Applications of Linguistics*. Edit. G.E. Perren and J.L.M. Trim. Cambridge.

Ferguson, C.A. and Morgan, R. (1959). Selected Readings in Applied Linguistics. *Linguistic Reporter*, Supplement 2.

Grauberg, W. (1971). An Error Analysis in German of First-year University Students In : *Applications of Linguistics*.

Halliday, M.A.K., McIntosh, A., Strevens, P. (1964). *The Linguistic Sciences and Language Teaching*. Longmans.

Hays, D.G. (1971). Applied Computational Linguistics In : *Applications of Linguistics*.

Ives, Sumner (1964). Linguistics in the Classroom. In : *Readings in Applied English Linguistics*. Edit. H.B. Allen. Amerind.

Krashen, S.D. (1982). *Principles and Practice in Second Language Acquisition*. Pergamon: New York.

Lado, Robert (1957). *Linguistics Across Cultures*. Ann Arbor.

Lehmann, W.P. (1970). Machine Translation. In. *Linguistics*. Edit. A.A. Hill. Higginbothams.

Lennon, Paul. (1988). The Linguist and the Language Teacher : Love at First Sight or The End of the Honeymoon. In *Forum*. Vol. XXVI, No. 4, October.

Malmberg, B. (1971). Applications of Linguistics. In: *Applications of Linguistics*.

Marckwardt, A.H. (1970) Linguistics and Instruction in the Native Language. In *Linguistics*.

Moulton, W.G. (1970). Linguistics. In : *The Aims and Methods of Scholarship in Modern Languages and Literatures*. A.S.R.C., Hyderabad.

Nickel, G. (1971). *Papers in Contrastive Linguistics*. Cambridge.

Patnaik, A. (1986). *Language and Thought Disorders Among Schizophrenics: A Structural Model for Linguistic Analysis*. M.D. Thesis. Ranchi University.

Pattanayak, D.P. (1984). Psycholinguistics in a Multilingual Society : New Directions for Research and Teaching. UGC National Seminar on Psycholinguistics.

Pit Corder, S. (1973). *Introducing Applied Linguistics*. Penguin.

Roberts, Paul. (1964). The Relation of Linguistics to the Teaching of English. In: *Readings in Applied English Linguistics*.

Siegel, J. (1980). Recent Developments in Linguistic Anthropology and Implication for Language Teaching. *Indian Journal of Applied Linguistics*. Vol. VI, No. 2, June.

Srivastava, R.N. (1985). Stylistics and the Teaching of Poetry. *Indian Journal of Applied Linguistics*, Vol. XI, No. 1, January.

Souvenir, National Seminar on Linguistics and Language Teaching. 1990. Department of Linguistics. Aligarh Muslim University.

Stern, H.H. (1983). *Fundamental Concepts of Language Teaching*. OUP.

Strain, J.E. (1971). A Recent Development in English Language Education in Japan : Materials Analysis. In : *Applications of Linguistics*.

Tosh, W. (1970). Computer Linguistics. In : *Linguistics*.

Verma, K. (1982). Linguistic Competence and Psychopathology : A Cross-cultural Model. Ind. Journ. Psychiat. 24.2.

Verma, S.K. (1975). Linguistics and Language Teaching. *Indian Linguistics*. Vol. 36, No. 3, September.

Verescagin, E.M. and Kostomarov, V.G. (1981). Linguocultural Studies: Linguistics and Methodology of Teaching Foreign Languages. *CIEFL* Bulletin, Vol. 17, No. 1.

Warfel, H.R. (1964). Dictionaries and Linguistics. In. *Readings in Applied English Linguistics*.

Whitaker, H. and Whitaker, H.A. (Edit.). (1976). *Studies in Neurolinguistics*, Vol. I, Academic Press.

Widdowson, H.G. (1980). Models and Fictions . *Applied Linguistics*, 1.2.

Wilkins, D.A. (1972). *Linguistics in Language Teaching, London* : Arnold.

10

A REGISTRAL VARIETY OF INDIAN ENGLISH

Even a casual look at an English newspaper published in India is bound to give the impression that it takes liberties with the English language. This is more obvious in the lexical field. In fact, the journalists have always been eccentric word-makers and experimenters in language and perhaps it is a matter of journalistic habit. One can prepare a long list of such "Indian" words. Here are a few of them: 'Bataidar' ("Bataidars attacked by farmers"—a headline in the *Indian Nations*, Patna, November 3, '74), 'Jotedar' ("Jotedars taking advantage of distress sale" — the *Statesman,* Calcutta, November 20, '74), 'Kisan' ("Kisan threat to stage dharna on rail track"—a headline in *the Times of India*, New Delhi, Feb. 5, '75), 'Mela' ("Mela like scene" — *the Indian Nation*, November 4, '74), 'Khaki' (a frequent use is 'Khaki shirts'), 'Ryot', 'Chaukidar' and 'Zamindar' (the word 'Zamindar' came to English in the seventeenth century). A research at the Central Institute of English and Foreign Languages, Hyderabad (1971) has also revealed that a distinctive feature of Indian news reporting is the use of a large number of words and expressions (Indianisms), peculiar to the socio-cultural situation obtaining in India. This tendency has been particularly noticeable during the last two decades though, of course, some of these words were in use even earlier. Undoubtedly it would be extremely interesting if we could find out who it was who used them first and when. But, to quote *Smith* (1966 : 56) "for the great majority of new words, even those created in the present day, such knowledge is unattainable." Usually these words do not possess, or soon lose, their 'birth-certificates'.

As one makes a close study of the Indianisms used in English newspapers and magazines published in India one finds that quite a large number of the more widely used ones are in one way or the other connected with violence, bloodshed or political movements. The present writer would like to draw the attention of the students of Indian English to this aspect. In this study proper nouns (*e.g.*, 'Gobar Gas') and italicized words or words used within inverted commas have not been taken into account.

It is proposed here to study the notable lexical items of this nature and also to refer to the actual uses of them in the newspapers and magazines by citing the typical ones. Only a few newspapers and magazines which were readily available were consulted and, also, only certain typical uses were put together for analysis. It was felt that the quotations thus collected were sufficient to throw light on the issue and also to lead to certain conclusions.

1. Of late, the use of 'bundh' (which is also spelt 'bund' and 'bandh') has remarkably increased. 'Bundh' actually means 'general strike' and when referring to a 'bundh' *the Times*, London (5-xi-1974) has used the expression 'general strike'. The *Times* actually describes the whole situation: "... stopped train services into the city and shut down schools and colleges and shops." Instead of explaining all this or using the expression 'general strike' an English newspaper published in India will readily use the single word 'Bund'. *The Mirror*, a magazine from Bombay, published (August '74) an article "How and why a Bundh is patriotic". "Three-day Bandh from October 3 planned in Bihar" was a headline in the *Statesman* on 28.ix.1974. The *Indian Nation* (1.x. 1974) carried headlines "Corner meetings in Bund support" and "3-day Bihar Bund will be non-violent". The *Patriot*, New Delhi, had as headlines. "Jodhpur bundh : 244 arrested (6.x.1974), "Bihar bundh toll rises to 15" (8.x. 1974), "Action against staff absent during bundh" (11.x.1974), "People asked to ignore November 4 bandh" (11.x.1974) and "DUTA split over bandh issue" (1.xi. 1974). The *Indian Nation* gave "Delhi University closed on Bund eve" as the headline (4.xi. 1974) of a news circulated by the Press Trust of India and "Buses plying on Bandh day" was the headline of a news (circulated by the same agency) in the *Statesman* (5.xi.1974). *The Hindustan Times*, New Delhi, contained a headline "Several towns observe bandh" (8.xi.1974). On the same date the *Amrita Bazar Patrika*, Calcutta, carried a headline "*Bihar bundh* passes off peacefully". "Bandh day in Delhi"...was the caption (10.xi.1974) of a photograph in the *Link* (a newsmagazine published from New Delhi). The *Indian Nation* (11.xi.1974) had a headline "Congress takes out massive

rally at bundh-bound Ranchi". "Kerala C.M. deplores bundh-call" was a headline in the *Statesman* (8.xii.1974). "Bandh threat by Gujarat industries" was a headline in the *Amrita Bazar Patrika* (9.xii.1974). *The Economic Times*, New Delhi, carried a headline "Call to ignore bandh" (15.1.1975). "Call for Patna bandh" was a headline in the *Hindustan Standard*, Calcutta (11.iii.1975). Incidentally, one of the topics for essay-writing in English II Paper in the annual intermediate examination '74 of Ranchi University was "The Recent 3-Day Bund in Bihar" and the idiom 'Colds bandh' appeared as the title of an advertisement of a rub for cold (in the *Indian Nation*, 14.ii.1975).

Expressions like 'bund-day', 'bund-call', bund-bound; and bund eve' are interesting compounds and reveal a noteworthy tendency.

2. Often we come across a direct mention of the lethal weapons still in use in India (It may be noted that the use of these terms was approved by English officers possessing Oxford and Cambridge degrees when proceedings in law courts were recorded during British rule in India). For instance, a news-item in the *Indian Nation* (12.xi.1974) carried this: "The demonstrators mostly barefooted villagers armed with various kinds of weapons including bows and arrows, spears, gadasas, bhalas, lathis etc...". The same newspaper in that very issue carried this sentence also : "They received either bhala or lathi injuries."

Perhaps these words are preferred because the reporters want to portray an exact picture of what had happened. Generally, it is also true that these terms do not have exact equivalents in English though 'spear' is the word for 'bircha'.

In "Advanced Learners" Dictionary (*ALD*) 'lathi' means long, iron-bound stick used as a weapon (by the police) in India'. *ALD* seems to be too conscious of the compound 'lathi-charge' which is, undeniably, in widespread use. To cite an instance, the *Statesman* had this headline (9.x.1974): "Lathi-charge at Srinagar". 'Lathi' is, however, not invariably used by the police alone. Kachru calls an expression like 'lathi-charge' 'a hybridized lexical item' (which is made up of two or more elements, at least one of which is from a South Asian language and one from English). 'Kotwali police', 'city kotwali', 'tank bund', 'ahimsa soldier', 'Shahid day' ect. are some other such hybridized forms. 'Police thana' and 'police station' are used interchangeably.

Let us examine the following examples: "Several persons also received lathi blows" — the *Indian Nation* (5.x.1974), "Large contingents of policemen tried to prevent people on the road from joining the procession by brandishing lathis"—the *Statesman* (5.xi.l974), his "arm was fractured while he was trying to save.... against police lathi blows"—the *Statesman* (8.xi.1974), "One would not like to imagine the consequences had the lathis fallen on the septuagenarian leader" — the *Statesman* (8.xi.1974), "... was hit by lathi-wielding police" — the *Statesman* (9.xi.1974), "I received lathi blow on November 4—XYZ"—the *Amrita Bazar Patrika* (16.11.1974) and "Tear-gas and lathis used to disperse Orissa teachers" — a headline in the *Statesman* (14.xii.1974). In all these instances, by 'lathi' is meant the 'lathis' carried by the police but certain other words which have actually been formed from 'lathi' *e.g.*, 'lathial' and 'lathait' do not, as a rule, refer to the lathis of the police. Though very occasionally, 'lathial' and 'lathait' also appear in our English newspapers. Probably the English word which comes nearest to giving an equivalent to the word 'lathi' is 'baton' which is (according to *ALD*) "policeman's short, thick stick, used as a weapon". whereas 'lathi' is "long iron-bound stick used as a weapon". Significantly, 'baton' is also to be seen in our newspapers off and on e.g., "violent mob baton-charged"— the *Indian Nation* (10.xi.1974). It seems probable that 'baton' referred to here is actually 'lathi'. On November 5, 1974 the *Times*, London also used 'baton' for 'lathi'.

3. Though not as often as 'bundh' the term 'bundobust' is also found in these newspapers. The *Indian Nation* writes in a news-item (circulated by the P.T.I.) on October 25, '74 "Alleged smuggler (X) was removed to the.....hospital....today in an ambulance under police bundobust." The *Indian Nation*, again, had this on 12.xi.1974 "....elaborate police bandobust had been made for maintaining peace......" "There was an unusually heavy police bundobust which gave the Kotla ground a look of a police camp" was a sentence in the same newspaper (13.xii.1974). 'Bundobust' is understandably not very widely used: it has good equivalents *e.g.*, 'arrangements'. It should be noted that Burke had used this term in connection with the examination of the political and commercial affairs of the East India Company. The year of its earliest known use in English in 1768 though *Oxford English Dictionary* (OED) recorded it for the first time in 1776.

4. One comes across the word 'dacoit' (də 'kə i t) in ALD where it means "member of a band of armed robbers (India, Burma)". The *Patriot* (12.x.1974) had a headline : "Dacoits loot running train". "5 arrested on charge of dacoity" was a headline in the *Indian Nation* (2.xi.l974). In the same newspaper "Alleged dacoit arrested" was a headline (4.xi.l974). The *Statesman* had a headline "Two shot dead by dacoits" (15.xi.1974). "Concern at dacoities in trains, buses" was a headline in the *Amrita Bazar Patrika* (21.xi. 1974) and "Dacoity bid fails" in the same newspaper (29.xi.1974). The nearest equivalent in English is an armed robber. It would be interesting to point out that in the *Indian Nation* of December 9, '74 a news had "Man stabbed to death by dacoits in running train" as the headline but the news itself referred to 'dacoit' as 'armed robber'. *English Pronouncing Dictionary* (*EPD*) and *OED* both have mentioned this word and also 'dacoitage' (which is out of fashion now). The word 'dacoit' appeared in English for the first time in 1810. 'Dacoity' ('gang robbery') was first recorded in 1848.

5. 'Dharna' is in popular use now-a-days though it is interesting to note that the word was first used in English in 1793. "... satyagrahis staging a dharna in front of the Old Secretariat in Patna" was the caption of a photograph in the *Statesman* (6.x. 1974). A headline in the *Indian Nation* (5.x.1974) was "XYZ to offer Dharna before Secretariat today". "School teachers' Dharna" (15.x.1974) and "Dharna against X's visit" (31.x.1974) were headlines in the *Patriot.* A news-item in the *Statesman* (9.xi. 1974) contained: "....by holding rallies, public meetings, dharnas, and demonstrations." A photograph in the *Link* (24.xi.1974) had "... on Dharna at Boat Club" as its caption. A headline in the *Hindustan Times* (12.xii.1974) read, "Dharna plan off".

'To squat' or 'to sit' can be used for 'Dharna' though if 'squat' is chosen it would not be possible to make such idioms as 'offering a dharna' and 'staging a dharna'. Sometimes we do find the use of the word 'squat' instead of 'dharna' though, one must concede, 'squat' does not possess the spirit of the word 'dharna'.

6. 'Gherao' is by far the most widely used of these words. The English equivalents to 'gherao' are 'surround' and 'siege'. "Half an hour siege of X's house' was a headline in the *Searchlight*, Patna, (6.xi.1974). The *Statesman* had a headline (25.xi.1974) : "(X) asks students to gherao AIR and to prevent by-elections." The same

news-item contained the word 'surround' in place of 'gherao': "There is no option left but to surround All India Radio and prevent it from functioning". Thus alongwith 'gherao' 'surround' and 'siege' are also occasionally used. *The Times*, London, also prefers 'besiege' (5.xi.1974) : "Riot police, using batons and tear gas, today foiled attempts by thousands of anti-corruption demonstrators to besiege Government offices and houses of ministers in the Bihar State capital of Patna".

The following are some typical uses of the word 'gherao' : "SP volunteers gherao (X)" — a headline in the *Indian Express*, New Delhi (2.ix.l974). "Women lift gherao of sugar producers" — a headline in the *Statesman* (28.ix.1974), "(X) was perhaps the most gherao'd man in Bombay" and "(X) is seen here being gherao'd" — captions of the photographs in the *Illustrated Weekly of India*, Bombay (29.ix.1974), "Vishwa Bharti V.C. under gherao"—a headline in the *Statesman* (8.x.1974) (The same news had "Vishwabharti V.C. gheraoed" as the headline in the *Patriot* (8.x.1974), 'B.L.D. plans to gherao Central Ministers"—a headline in the *Statesman* (9.x.1974), "(X) announces gherao of Secretariat on Nov. 4"—a headline in *The Times of India*, New Delhi (13.x.1974), "Govt. set to foil Nove. 4 gherao" — a headline in the *Indian Nation* (2.xi.1974), "Massive gherao of Parliament, AIR planned"—a headline in the *Statesman* (25.xi.1974), "Women gherao Dy. Commissioner at Jharia" (25.xi.1974), and "Parliament House gherao planned" (27.xi.1974), headlines in the *Amrita Bazar Patrika* and "Gherao denied" a headline in the *Indian Nation* (16.xii.1974), *The Shankar's Weekly*, New Delhi (Annual 1974) had an article entitled "In praise of gherao". The caption of a photograph in the fortnightly *Caravan*, New Delhi, was "The people showed their discontent by organizing bandhs, gheraos, and agitations". Orient Longmans Ltd. has recently published Sujata Dasgupta's book *The Great Gherao of 1969. Gherao* is the title of a well-known short-story written by Arun Joshi in English.

7. 'Goonda' means a hooligan or a rogue or a scoundrel. Till a few years ago our newspapers had a peculiar predilection for this term. (Examples : "Some goondas arrested" and "the goonda elements rounded up"). Though no longer a favourite with the journalists the word continues to make occasional appearances. "Sometimes, Workers' Unions are run with the help of rowdies and goondas" was the caption of a photograph in the *Caravan*

(1.11.1975) ".... hiring goondas to assault some employees" was the part of a sentence in a news-item in the *Indian Nation* (23.iii. 1975). The term is now used in a different style also. A news-item in the *Indian Nation* (12.xi.1974) contained : ".... condemned XYZ for introducing lathis and goondas in Bihar politics."

Surprisingly, the use of this word in English has begun only in the twentieth century. To hazard a guess, the word 'goonda' seems to be related to 'Goon' which, as described in the *Standard Dictionary of the English Language* (*SDEL*), is a U.S. slang. The first meaning of this word as given by the Dictionary (The Standard Dictionary of the English Language combined with Britannica World Language Dictionary, Vol. I, 1959 Reprint), is "a roughneck; thug; specially, one employed during labour disputes; most commonly used in the phrase 'goon squad'. According to the 1964 Reprint of the *Concise Oxford Dictionary* (COD) 'goon' is a person hired by racketeers to terrorise workers". The Marathi *gunda* is at least as old as the seventeenth century and may be of Dravidian origin.

8. Till recently the use of the word 'hartal' was in vogue. In any case, however, the same cannot be said about it now. Though it seems the word has fallen out of grace it is not in absolute disuse either. 'Hartal' has got an appropriate equivalent in English *i.e.*, 'strike'. In *ALD* the word means "(in India) closing of shops as a mark of sorrow or for a political reason" and in *SDEL* it means "In India, a suspension or stopping of business, as a form of mourning or passive protest against a political measure or situation" (one should perhaps mention at this point that *COD* has described the world 'hartal' as a blended form of two Hindustani words, 'hat' *i.e.* 'shop' and 'tala' which means 'lock'). This meaning does not appear to by very accurate because when shops are closed as a mark of sorrow or a form of mourning it is, strictly speaking, not a 'hartal' and the 'hartal' does not mean only closing of shops either *e.g.*, employees also observe 'hartal' to press their demands. According to *ALD* the pronunciation of the word is ('ha: ta: 1). *SDEL* takes note of the /r/ sound /hār-tā 1/. *COD* gives (hārt 'a) which is not used in India at all. The Hindustani pronunciation is of course hər tal with a flap and an end-stress. *The Searchlight* contained this headline (6.xi. 1974) : "Patna observes complete hartal" and the *Statesman* had "Bhutto's Kashmir Hartal Call Amounts to Meddling" as a headline (17.ii.1975). Obviously at least the *Searchlight* wanted to refer to a 'bund'. To be exact there is not much of a difference between a

The exact sets of semantic components of the language are no doubt significant but the translator is supposed to see how these components fit into 'the much broader communicative patterns of the language'—'how what is said fits into what is not said' (Nida : 1971). For instance, while translating idioms, 'the sets of semantic components must be entirely redistributed'. 'An analysis of functional roles of different participants' (Arya : 1974) can bring out useful facts. A bilingual or multilingual who possesses two or several grammars (Smith and Wilson : 1975, Chomsky : 1975) cannot wholly depend on his intuition in this matter. Catford (1965) thinks that a text can be analysed in terms of contextually relevant situational features. Catford calls them situational distinctive features. 'In the same way that the surgeon operating on the heart cannot neglect the body that surrounds it, so the translator treats the text in isolation from the culture, at his peril'—(McGuire : 1980 : 14). In the English tradition 'taking off hat from one's head' is a symbol of showing respect whereas in the Indian context 'taking off turban/ cap' from one's head is a mark of disrespect.

Therefore, the communicative equivalence and the different stylistic and registral variations of both the source language (SL) and the target language (TL) should be borne in mind while translating because the translator will be called upon to make the appropriate syntactic and lexical adjustments. One's early step, therefore, should always be to indentify the register in the SL text. The translator should not be oblivious of the language varieties like regional dialect, temporal dialect, class dialect, idiolect etc. Ulrych (1986) mentions the Italian *Voto* which will be translated as *vow* in religious register, as *vote* in political register and *mark* when referring to academic performance. The Italian *accusare* may simply mean *accuse* but in a legal register it may mean *charge* and in medical register *to feel*. It has been found that English words tends to be polysemous and Japanese words tend to be monosemous. As we study the following, we find "cold" in all the English sentences but the corresponding Japanese sentences do not share any one word:

Cold

English	*Japanese*
I feel *cold*	*samuke*-ga suru
It is *cold*	*samui*

cold soft drinks	*tsumetai* nomimono
I've caught (a) *cold*	*Kaze*-o hiita

The same goes for *hot* :

English	*Japanese*
I feel *hot*	*netsuppoi*
It is *hot*	*atsui*
hot water	*netto* (or *atsui* yu)

A person who knows that 'tour' means 'a package tour' will be surprised when asked (in Japan), "Would you take a tour of our house?"

The constraints of collocation should not be lost sight of as, otherwise, situations may become rather comic, *e.g.*, 'The tea is too light for me' in Indian English. Ulrych (1986) talks of the Italian verb *dichiarare* which may be translated into English in a number of ways *e.g.*, *lo dichiararo suo erede*—he made him his heir; *vi dichiararo marito e moglie*—I pronounce you man and wife; *nulla da dichiarare*—nothing to declare. It is the translator's job to decide from the linguistic and situational contexts whether in Italian *I suoi ochhi brillarono*—his/her eyes glistened with tears, flashed with indignation or sparkled with joy. Ulrych (1986) shows the wide range of possible equivalents for *rubare* with the help of the following stylistic scale displaying the degree of formality:

Slang	Colloquial		informal		formal
rip off	snitch	swipe	lift pinch	steal	pilfer

The Vende Bible used for a long time the term *pfumedzanya* for 'reconcile' in passages which speak of God 'reconciling the world to himself' whereas the term literally means 'let someone become rich at another's expense'. The Bible talks about 'separating the sheep from the goats' on the day of judgement and we need not explain that sheep stand for favourite persons whereas goats symbolize the opposite. A translation like this, however, will simply upset people in Central Africa where goats are highly prized and sheep serve as almost 'despised scavengers'. When 'Hell' is described as 'a place where the fire never goes out', the people of West Africa feel attracted towards it, as their idea of a bad place would be a cold place and not a hot one.

Lehmann (1970) and Verma (1978) have rightly suggested that conventional expressions and expressions used as phatic communion are best translated by the equivalent conventions in the other language, substituted mechanically and not by looking at the meanings of the constituents. Otherwise, the things would look strange and ridiculous. The German greeting *Guten Tag* should be translated as 'Hello' in English because the exact English translation of *Guten Tag i.e.* 'good day' would simply be laughable. The same would be the effect of the Japanese expression, *Sayonara*, if it is translated as *if it must be so* and not as 'Good Bye'. The Italian word *ciao* is used as a form of greeting equally on arrival and departure. Even the English expressions *Good Morning*, *Good Afternoon* and *Good Evening* etc. have no exact equivalents in Hindi and other Indian languages. The Hindi greeting term *Namaste* can serve all these purposes. In much the same way, the English expression 'How do you do' is culture bound. Its literal translation in Hindi *i.e. tum kis tarah karte ho* has an entirely different sense.

A machine translation will be crude and brutally honest and that is why it often makes us laught. A word-for-word or rank bound translation results in humorous situations. The Hindi translation of English sentence 'It's raining cats and dogs' as *kutte aur billiyaN baras rahe haiN* will be rank bound and just a mockery. The simple German sentence *Diese kurze gemeinsame Ueberlegung ist eine art experiment mit uns selbst gewesen* is a long sentence and translating longer sentences gives rise to more complex problems and produces more laughable situations. In this sentence the most serious problem is the position of the verb. The appropriate translation should be 'The short joint reflection has been a kind of experiment with ourselves' and not 'has a kind of joint experiment with ourselves been.' The German expression *Uns selbst* is translated *ourselves* and not *us self*. The English verb *go* has a certain meaning in sentences like 'He's going home' though in 'He's going steady' the verb has an absolutely different meaning *i.e.*, 'being in love'. In 'He had to go', 'go' may carry several entirely different shades of meaning. The translation of trick sentences or ambiguous sentences often creates difficulties. Tosh (1970) has drawn our attention to the difficulties in the treatment of 'discontinuity' and cites as an example 'Will you look the list over?' When a speaker in the United Nations quoted this excerpt from the Bible, 'The spirit is willing but the flesh is weak' the computer translated it into other languages as 'The wine is good but the meat is bad'.

Many in India translate the Hindi sentence *aap kya karte haiN, Lal Sahib*? as 'What you do, Mr. Lal?. Since there is hardly anything like indirect form of narration in Hindi our people often come out with translations like 'Do you know where does he live?'. In English in India, as an impact of the first language, the tag is almost always 'isn't it' or 'no', whatever the main question. When they produce such translations as 'your both hands are dirty', 'my all friends are here' and 'this my friend is very poor', the word order in the SL is generally the cause.

Translation in a literal style results in a number of typical errors of article in India as there is no article worthy of the name in Indian languages. Also, translations like 'I am seeing a man outside' are very common in our country because such an expression is close to our usage although, as we know, 'see' and a few other verbs are seldom used in continuous form. It may be interesting to quote Dr. Amarnath Jha here : 'Who is there in the United Provinces who does not know freeship? All of us know what a student means when he says that he is engaged in *teachery* and soon hopes to get *headmastery*. Must we insist on *all this* when *this all* is nearer our own usage?' It is because of Hindi that in reply to 'Aren't you coming to dinner tonight?' many say 'Yes, I am not' or 'No, I am coming'. There is no concord, as can be easily noticed, between the two parts of the sentences here. The correct English equivalents should be 'No, I am not' or 'Yes, of course, I'm'.

The translator who comes out with 'I wented there yesterday' does so on the analogy of 'wanted', 'parted' etc. On the analogy of 'the above statement' he generates 'the below statement.' A translation like 'After abusing me he left saying he would see me outside the college' may be unintelligible to the native speakers of English whereas 'The warden reached in time and cooled the matter' and 'you cannot get a good job without some source' may be unacceptable to them. When asked to explain what they understood by the expression 'Her face-cut is very impressive' in a translated passage, some native speakers of English came out with rather amusing interpretations—She has good bones; her hair-cut is very impressive; her facial scar is very striking; she cut her face badly, poor girl; it sounds as though she has been in a fight with knife cuts; and does the girl shave?

'complete hartal' and a 'bund'. Hence the slump in the use of the word 'hartal'.

9. The word 'Satyagraha' was recorded by the OED in 1921 and was used by Aldous Huxley in 1928. Though the word was never completely out of sight it is once again in wide use in the newspapers these days. 'Satya' means truth and 'agraha' stands for insistence. Thus the word means 'insistance on truth' and 'satyagrahi' is the person who practises satyagraha. A headline in the *Indian Nation* read (4.xi.1974): He "asks satyagrahis to remain peaceful". In the *Statesman* there were the headlines : "satyagrahi prisoners lathi-charged" (8.xi.1974); "satyagrah put off till Monday" (7.xii.1974). "Satyagrah threat" (9.xii.1974) and "Satyagrah stalemate" (19.xii. 1974) were headlines in the *Amrita Bazar Patrika*. A photograph in the *Caravan* had "(X) addressing the *Dharna* satyagrahis" as its caption (11.xii.1974).

10. Certain other Hindustani terms of this nature are also often used in these newspapers. 'Naxalite' is a term which, in the words of *The Times*. London, "came into use after a Maoist type peasant uprising in the Naxalbari area of Northern West Bengal in 1967" (*Times*, 17.ix.1974) 'Naxalite' (also 'Naxalism') was a vogue word in the later sixties and is in large scale circulation even now. Occasionally, one comes across 'zoolum' or 'zulm' *i.e.* 'tyranny' or oppression'. To cite an instance : "(X) alleges police zoolum"..... was a headline in the *Indian Nation* of Feb. 5, '75. 'Loot', 'Kotwali', 'Hajat', and 'Jawan' etc. are some other such words. It is important that the English news-readers of All India Radio also use these as also a number of other expressions. For example, the English news bulletin at 9.15 P.M. on 4.xi.1974 contained the word 'gherao', 'bund', 'lathi-charge' and 'dharna'.

It should be emphasized here that English has borrowed some words from German military vocabulary (during and after the Second World War). Also, it has borrowed 'Guerillas' and 'Commandos' and other words with regard to war from some other languages. Subba Rao (1954) has drawn our attention to *Ahimsa, Badmash, Bundook, Darogah, Foujdar, Jamadar, Phansigar, Sowar, Thug* and *Zindabad*. In fact, the word 'Kotwal' came to English in the seventeenth century (1623). A recent edition of *The Random House Dictionary of the English Language* includes 'ahimsa', 'kotwal'; 'goonda', 'thana', 'topkhana' and 'jawan'. *The Little Oxford Dictionary of Current English* (1977) has a supplement of 1500 Indian words listed by R.E. Hawkins. It may be worth mentioning in passing that British novelists have made use of a number of the Indianisms discussed in this article. Almost all the words taken up in this study have, as has already been discussed, equivalents or near-equivalents in the English language though maybe these expressions do not convey the precise nuances conveyed by the Hindustani ones. Perhaps it is not possible to use several of these English equivalents in the way these newspapers have used the Hindustani words. But then the English substitutes can also be used in a number of other ways. For instance, they cannot say "staging or offering a squat or squatting" in the way they say "staging or offering a dharna" but they can say 'squatted' whereas 'dharnad' has not been used yet (though 'gheraod' has been). Then why do the Indian newspapers, magazines, and All India Radio news-readers tend to use these deviations repeatedly? It is really difficult to furnish a palatable explanation. Subba Rao has rightly observed (1966 : 27): "India's struggle for independence and the unique methods adopted for its achievement are indicated by such words as *Gandhism, hartal, Khaddar, Khilafat Satyagraha, Swadeshi* and *Swaraj*—all faithfully recorded by the 'OED.'" Perhaps the reason is that the journalists try to use what has been called *LME* (Locally Modified English). Of course, these newspapers cater to the needs of the 'general' reading public and thus it is—natural that they aim at creating an atmosphere not 'remote' from them. That is why (it seems) these words are more widely used in the local and regional newspapers (though the national press is also not free from these). It is also possible that they use these words for the sake of 'economy' because generally such a term reduces a cumbrous descriptive expression to one word. Naturally more words will be required if the description of a 'bund' or a 'satyagrah' is preferred and to my mind this explains why these terms are found mostly in headlines.

As noted earlier, some of these words appear in *OED, EPD, COD, SDEL*, and *ALD* etc. Thus we can guess that the native speakers of English largely understand them. Quirk (1967 : 96) also maintains that any native user of English can read a newspaper printed in Delhi without difficulty and often even without realising that there are differences at all. *Glossary of Judicial and Revenue Terms (1855)* compiled by Wilson and *Hobson-Jobson : A Glossary of Colloquial Anglo-Indian Words and Phrases, and of Kindred Terms, Etymological, Historical, Geographical and Discursive* compiled by Yule and Burnell (1886) were early attempts to compile lexical lists of this kind. But, surprisingly enough, Potter (1969) and Foster (1972) did not care to make a mention of any of the words discussed here. The hospitality extended by English to words from other languages has, in fact, never been in question. But, interestingly, Foster (1972 : 72) has himself said, "This may be annoying to the purist". Smith has put it in his own way (1966 : 64): "(English language) has been mutilated as hardly any other language has been mutilated, but these mutilations have made place for wonderful new growths". The fact remains, however, that only a few Indian words have found their way into the native varieties of English.

The point to be stressed here is that proper attention should be paid to this registral variety of Indian English.

REFERENCES

Foster, B. 1972, *The Changing English Language*. St. Martins Press: Macmillan.

Kachru, Braj B. 1978. Lexical Innovations in South Asian English, In : Mohan, Ramesh (ed.) *Indian Writing in English*, Madras : Orient Longman.

Potter, Simeon, 1969. *Changing English*, London : Deutsch (Andre) Ltd.

Quirk, R. 1967. *The Use of English*, London : Longman.

Smith, L.P. 1966. *The English Language*, London : OUP.

Subba Rao, G. 1954. *Indian Words in English*, London : OUP (1969 impression used).

11

HUMOUR AND TRANSLATION : EVIDENCE FROM INDIAN ENGLISH

'The Railway does not belong to your father', 'Where have you gone and died?', 'Does my lap bite you?', 'No one can stop anyone's mouth' are statements made by characters in certain Indian novels in English. Translators, in fact, often literally translate oft-repeated Indianisms. When translation from one language into another is attempted, certain things occasionally show oddities and discrepancies. Sometimes such odd uses heighten artistic effect, enhance realistic tinge or produce comic situations. Many of them, however, are there because of ignorance. Untranslatability (linguistic, cultural and collocational) also frequently confronts a translator.

Roland Barthes once said he absolutely refused to translate anything (Diot : 1986 : 185). Talking of homour, in particular, Diot (1986) finds the operation a desperate one—'while the denotations can roughly be translated into a different language, the connotations cannot. They resist the process of exportation and perish in the shipping'. Robert Graves calls translation 'a lie', 'a polite lie'. Translators, it may be interesting to recall here, have also been labelled as 'traitors'. Undoubtedly, literal meanings are often notoriously inadequate guides to actual usage (Nida : 1971). The socio-cultural and economic backgrounds of the respective areas, in many cases, produce baffling though amusing predicaments. That is why, both the deep and surface structures should be taken note of. The French translator, E. Dolet was, as we gather, strangulated to death and all his writings put to flame as his translation of Plato was considered to be unfaithful to the original. Faithful translations, it goes without saying, are seldom useful.

The exact sets of semantic components of the language are no doubt significant but the translator is supposed to see how these components fit into 'the much broader communicative patterns of the language'—'how what is said fits into what is not said' (Nida : 1971). For instance, while translating idioms, 'the sets of semantic components must be entirely redistributed'. 'An analysis of functional roles of different participants' (Arya : 1974) can bring out useful facts. A bilingual or multilingual who possesses two or several grammars (Smith and Wilson : 1975, Chomsky : 1975) cannot wholly depend on his intuition in this matter. Catford (1965) thinks that a text can be analysed in terms of contextually relevant situational features. Catford calls them situational distinctive features. 'In the same way that the surgeon operating on the heart cannot neglect the body that surrounds it, so the translator treats the text in isolation from the culture, at his peril'—(McGuire : 1980 : 14). In the English tradition 'taking off hat from one's head' is a symbol of showing respect whereas in the Indian context 'taking off turban/cap' from one's head is a mark of disrespect.

Therefore, the communicative equivalence and the different stylistic and registral variations of both the source language (SL) and the target language (TL) should be borne in mind while translating because the translator will be called upon to make the appropriate syntactic and lexical adjustments. One's early step, therefore, should always be to indentify the register in the SL text. The translator should not be oblivious of the language varieties like regional dialect, temporal dialect, class dialect, idiolect etc. Ulrych (1986) mentions the Italian *Voto* which will be translated as *vow* in religious register, as *vote* in political register and *mark* when referring to academic performance. The Italian *accusare* may simply mean *accuse* but in a legal register it may mean *charge* and in medical register *to feel*. It has been found that English words tends to be polysemous and Japanese words tend to be monosemous. As we study the following, we find "cold" in all the English sentences but the corresponding Japanese sentences do not share any one word:

Cold

English	*Japanese*
I feel *cold*	*samuke*-ga suru
It is *cold*	*samui*

cold soft drinks	*tsumetai* nomimono
I've caught (a) *cold*	*Kaze*-o hiita

The same goes for *hot* :

English	*Japanese*
I feel *hot*	*netsuppoi*
It is *hot*	*atsui*
hot water	*netto* (or *atsui* yu)

A person who knows that 'tour' means 'a package tour' will be surprised when asked (in Japan), "Would you take a tour of our house?"

The constraints of collocation should not be lost sight of as, otherwise, situations may become rather comic, *e.g.*, 'The tea is too light for me' in Indian English. Ulrych (1986) talks of the Italian verb *dichiarare* which may be translated into English in a number of ways *e.g.*, *lo dichiararo suo erede*—he made him his heir; *vi dichiararo marito e moglie*—I pronounce you man and wife; *nulla da dichiarare*—nothing to declare. It is the translator's job to decide from the linguistic and situational contexts whether in Italian *I suoi ochhi brillarono*—his/her eyes glistened with tears, flashed with indignation or sparkled with joy. Ulrych (1986) shows the wide range of possible equivalents for *rubare* with the help of the following stylistic scale displaying the degree of formality:

Slang	Colloquial		informal		formal
rip off	snitch	swipe	lift pinch	steal	pilfer

The Vende Bible used for a long time the term *pfumedzanya* for 'reconcile' in passages which speak of God 'reconciling the world to himself' whereas the term literally means 'let someone become rich at another's expense'. The Bible talks about 'separating the sheep from the goats' on the day of judgement and we need not explain that sheep stand for favourite persons whereas goats symbolize the opposite. A translation like this, however, will simply upset people in Central Africa where goats are highly prized and sheep serve as almost 'despised scavengers'. When 'Hell' is described as 'a place where the fire never goes out', the people of West Africa feel attracted towards it, as their idea of a bad place would be a cold place and not a hot one.

Lehmann (1970) and Verma (1978) have rightly suggested that conventional expressions and expressions used as phatic communion are best translated by the equivalent conventions in the other language, substituted mechanically and not by looking at the meanings of the constituents. Otherwise, the things would look strange and ridiculous. The German greeting *Guten Tag* should be translated as 'Hello' in English because the exact English translation of *Guten Tag i.e.* 'good day' would simply be laughable. The same would be the effect of the Japanese expression, *Sayonara*, if it is translated as *if it must be so* and not as 'Good Bye'. The Italian word *ciao* is used as a form of greeting equally on arrival and departure. Even the English expressions *Good Morning*, *Good Afternoon* and *Good Evening* etc. have no exact equivalents in Hindi and other Indian languages. The Hindi greeting term *Namaste* can serve all these purposes. In much the same way, the English expression 'How do you do' is culture bound. Its literal translation in Hindi *i.e. tum kis tarah karte ho* has an entirely different sense.

A machine translation will be crude and brutally honest and that is why it often makes us laught. A word-for-word or rank bound translation results in humorous situations. The Hindi translation of English sentence 'It's raining cats and dogs' as *kutte aur billiyaN baras rahe haiN* will be rank bound and just a mockery. The simple German sentence *Diese kurze gemeinsame Ueberlegung ist eine art experiment mit uns selbst gewesen* is a long sentence and translating longer sentences gives rise to more complex problems and produces more laughable situations. In this sentence the most serious problem is the position of the verb. The appropriate translation should be 'The short joint reflection has been a kind of experiment with ourselves' and not 'has a kind of joint experiment with ourselves been.' The German expression *Uns selbst* is translated *ourselves* and not *us self*. The English verb *go* has a certain meaning in sentences like 'He's going home' though in 'He's going steady' the verb has an absolutely different meaning *i.e.*, 'being in love'. In 'He had to go', 'go' may carry several entirely different shades of meaning. The translation of trick sentences or ambiguous sentences often creates difficulties. Tosh (1970) has drawn our attention to the difficulties in the treatment of 'discontinuity' and cites as an example 'Will you look the list over?' When a speaker in the United Nations quoted this excerpt from the Bible, 'The spirit is willing but

the flesh is weak' the computer translated it into other languages as 'The wine is good but the meat is bad'.

Many in India translate the Hindi sentence *aap kya karte haiN, Lal Sahib*? as 'What you do, Mr. Lal?. Since there is hardly anything like indirect form of narration in Hindi our people often come out with translations like 'Do you know where does he live?'. In English in India, as an impact of the first language, the tag is almost always 'isn't it' or 'no', whatever the main question. When they produce such translations as 'your both hands are dirty', 'my all friends are here' and 'this my friend is very poor', the word order in the SL is generally the cause.

Translation in a literal style results in a number of typical errors of article in India as there is no article worthy of the name in Indian languages. Also, translations like 'I am seeing a man outside' are very common in our country because such an expression is close to our usage although, as we know, 'see' and a few other verbs are seldom used in continuous form. It may be interesting to quote Dr. Amarnath Jha here : 'Who is there in the United Provinces who does not know freeship? All of us know what a student means when he says that he is engaged in *teachery* and soon hopes to get *headmastery*. Must we insist on *all this* when *this all* is nearer our own usage?' It is because of Hindi that in reply to 'Aren't you coming to dinner tonight?' many say 'Yes, I am not' or 'No, I am coming'. There is no concord, as can be easily noticed, between the two parts of the sentences here. The correct English equivalents should be 'No, I am not' or 'Yes, of course, I'm'.

The translator who comes out with 'I wented there yesterday' does so on the analogy of 'wanted', 'parted' etc. On the analogy of 'the above statement' he generates 'the below statement.' A translation like 'After abusing me he left saying he would see me outside the college' may be unintelligible to the native speakers of English whereas 'The warden reached in time and cooled the matter' and 'you cannot get a good job without some source' may be unacceptable to them. When asked to explain what they understood by the expression 'Her face-cut is very impressive' in a translated passage, some native speakers of English came out with rather amusing interpretations—She has good bones; her hair-cut is very impressive; her facial scar is very striking; she cut her face badly, poor girl; it sounds as though she has been in a fight with knife cuts; and does the girl shave?

As Arya (1974) has shown through analysis of translated passages, even the translation of a preposition 'to' in 'to a bridge' may cause difficulties. It may be difficult to decide whether the proper translation (in Hindi) is *tak, ke pas* or *par*. If *voh London gya* is translated into English as "He went London', it may be because of the Hindi version which, literally speaking, will be 'He London went' in English. 'To' does not have any equivalent in the Hindi sentence here. Luckily, we do not come across many mistakes of this nature. The Hindi 'se' is expressed both by 'for' and 'since' without realizing that their occurrence is rule-governed. 'Going by walk' is a common use in South India perhaps on the analogy of 'going by car' and 'going by bus' etc. During an experiment conducted by the present writer, a student came out with 'They look at very beautiful'. The fact that many of these prepositions have a number of meanings—'of' has 63 meanings listed in the Oxford English Dictionary—further complicates the job of a translator. H.G. Wells asks whether or not the Chinese language has a grammar. Where a sensible Englishman would remark, "Why walk in the ancient ways?" Wells gives the Chinese equivalent as "affairs, query, imperative, old". The literalness of the observation gave Wells another mistaken opinion that Chinese is also devoid of metaphor (1961 : 121).

Sometimes new lexical items are needed to talk about things and thought processes for which there are no equivalents or near equivalents in the TL. English does not have equivalents of Hindi *Kal* and *parsoN*. *Kal* may be used for yesterday or tomorrow whereas *parsoN* may mean 'the day after tomorrow' 'or 'the day before yesterday.' The kinship terminologies of SL and TL particularly make the task of a translator difficult. For instance, 'co-brother' or 'co-brother-in-law' has a culturally determined value in our country. There is only one word 'uncle' in English for our *chacha, tau, mama, phoopha, mousa* or *khaloo* and only one word '*aunt*' for *chachi, tai, mami,* or *mamani* and *mousi* or *khala*. The English 'brother-in-law, has two equivalents in Hindi, *jija* or *bahnoi* and *sala*. The words 'colony,' 'prepone' and 'almirah' etc. as used in India may appear rather arbitrary to a native speaker of English. The same may be said about expressions like 'bread of illegality', 'pin-drop silence' and 'your good name' etc. When 'bus' is used for 'coach', 'latrine' for 'toilet' and 'marketing' for 'shopping' they certainly look arbitrary. As there is only one lexical item in Hindi for both 'fingers' and 'toes' *i.e. ungli*, we find translations like 'leg fingers' and 'hand fingers.'

Reduplicative words which occur extensively in Indian languages in a variety of semantic functions often produce hilarious situations in exact translations. The underlined verbs in the following sentences are in their reduplicated structures of present imperfect, past perfect and gerundive forms respectively (Abbi : 1977) :

(i) vo calte calte gir paRaa
he walking waling fell down
He fell down while he was walking

(ii) Zaid kursi par baithe baithc thak gaya
Zaid chair in sitting sitting got tired
Zaid got tired of sitting in the chair (for too long).

(iii) maaN ne ro ro kar apna dukhRa Sunaaya
mother crying crying her grief told
Crying, the mother told about her grief.

Some other examples :

— Shyam ke dekhte dekhte (seeing seeing) Radha kamre meN ghusi.

— Hari paan bacte bacte (selling selling) buDDha ho gaya.

— maeN baat kahte kahte (saying saying) mk gaya.

— tum khaana khaate khaate (eating eating) mat bola karo.

It is particularly interesting to note that whereas *moti moti aankheN* is a compliment the expressions like *mote mote chor* convey a thoroughly different image. Sometimes we find translations like 'we saw mam good good things' (achhi achhi cheezeN) and 'My heart became garden garden (baagh baagh) when I saw him' (The appropriate translation should be 'my joy knew no bounds when I saw him'). A repetition of a particular word often shows change in meaning 'Sate, sate' (Is that so? in English) is an expression of astonishment in Oriya.

In Tamil (in South India) the people generally avoid making a statement like 'I'm going' because, as they perhaps apprehend, it may mean 'going from this world'. Tamil speakers, therefore, use expressions like 'I'm going and coming' instead of plain 'I'm going'. Consequently, English translations from Tamil often carry such uses. The tendency to translate the Oriya sentence *mo pakhaare kichi paise* naahi into English as 'I have no money near me' shows that the translator uses the system of Oriya for the system of English.

Indian writers in English have innovated translation equivalents to present the thought processes that cannot be adequately translated in a foreign language idiom. Verma (1978) goes to the extent of saying that in some cases they are bad translations. Instead of saying 'nip it in the bud', Raja Rao, in a characteristically Indian way, has said, 'crush in the seed'. 'As if you were cattle/animal/beast' is a transliterated Indianism. When Raja Rao uses expressions like 'like a noble cow', 'as a first-calved cow' and 'helpless as a calf' he is actually translating equivalents in Indian languages into English. 'Ah, this cat has taken to asceticism' (*Kanthapura*, Raja Rao) is in reality a famous Indian saying. 'You go like a fish hooked on a string' and 'his touch could turn mud into gold' in Arun Joshi's *The Strange Case of Billy Biswas* and *The Last Labyrinth* respectively have sprung from Indian usage. 'Large eyes were like a lake after a rain' (*The Foreigner*, Joshi) and the description of Jahanara's hair in Anita Desai's *Voices in the City* as that 'cloud of black hair swaying about the body' have been virtually transliterated. Bhattacharya talks of 'each grain a grain of gold' (in *So Many Hungers* !) and Raja Rao wants the rice to be as fine as a filigree (in *Kanthapura*). Ahmed Ali remarks, in *Ocean of Night*: 'Nawab looked as if he had won the pearls of the seven seas'. In the same novel, the picture of the fickleness of fortune has been borrowed straight from the vernacular—'how fickle is fortune more than a woman's heart, Talking of fortune, once again, Ali says, 'Fortune is fickle like the moon which lasts but only four days.' Ali presents 'desire' as 'restless like a moth around the flame.' This, once again, is almost a literal translation of a well-known Urdu expression *i.e.*, 'Shama' and 'Parwana.' The Indian habit of spitting or suggesting spitting to emphasize one's hatred of something or to abuse or ridicule the thing or to show atrocities or an emphatic denial or disapproval of something has been readily translated into English by these writers.

Another aspect of the Indian speech habit is that money is frequently used for comparison. Also, often there are hyperboilc numerical assertions. They are often transliterated that way by these writers. Time and again such instances produce humorous effect:

— I will draw a hundred lines on the earth with the tip of my nose (*Coolie*, Anand).

— the wife of a hundred husbands (*Two Leaves and a Bud*, Anand).
— The saying is worth a hundred thousand rupees (*Train to Pakistan*, Khushwant Singh).
— Whatever you say is right to the sixteenth anna of a rupee (*Train to Pakistan*, Khushwant Singh).
— Why do you torment me with the cucumber for the dozenth time (*The Dark Room*, Narayan).

Certain verbs as used by these writers appear transliterated from Indian languages. 'You have been eating my cars' (*Train to Pakistan*), 'You don't eat my head' and 'I will take you to eat a little fresh air' (*Coolie*), 'I hear that the girl has rolled many papads' and 'You have cut my nose bitch' (*Old Woman and the Cow*, Anand) are interesting expressions. It may not be irrelevant to quote Anand (1969) here: 'I generally translate or interpret my feelings or thoughts from Punjabi or Hindustani into the English language thus translating the metaphor and imagery of my mother tongue into what is called Indo-Anglo-Indian writing, but what I prefer to call 'pigeon Indian' (not 'Pidgin Indian'). Verma (1980) feels that as translation equivalents of corresponding expressions in Indian languages, they are highly idiosyncratic and arbitrary. Verma tries to substantiate his assertion by citing the following examples from Anand's fiction:

— my counterfeit luck (mera khota naseeb).
— is this any talk? (yeh bhi koi baat hui).
— nothing black in the pulse (daal meN kaala).
— made my sleep illegal (neend haraam kar diya).

Many of the 'interesting' abuses and admonitions have been plainly translated from the peculiar Indian (or even regional) day-to-day conversations. For example, 'lover of thy own sister' (*Ocean of Night*, Ahmed Ali), 'Ohe this Gandhi, would he were destroyed' (*Kanthapura*), 'Oh, come on public hair' and 'son of a black Shaitan' (*A Bend in the Ganges*, Malgonkar) etc. Animalification has been often used for this purpose as is often done in India: 'You cannot straighten a dog's tail' (*Kanthapura*), 'Munoo followed him like a dog behind his master' (*Coolie*), 'ari ari, bitch ! Do you take me for a buffoon' (*Untouchable*, Anand), Curly spoke like an ass' (*Two*

Virgins, Markandaya) and 'he began to climb up like a monkey' (*Maria*, Abbas).

Indian writers in English translate phrases, sayings and proverbs, too. These are generally the products of a particular culture. That is why, an attempt should be made to have semantic equivalents. For example, 'My head is eating circles' for the Hindi expressions: *mera sar chakkar kha raha hae* (My head circles eating) :

— you haven't the strength to kill an ant and will fight an elephant (*Ocean of Night*).

— Toba, toba, kill my own village banian, Babuji, who kills a hen which lays eggs (*Train to Pakistan*).

— He who has the big stick will have the buffalo (*Death of a Hero*, Anand).

— He was as yet essentially a pawn on the chessboard of destiny (*Coolie*).

— Bathe your feet while the Ganges still flows (*A Bend in the Ganges*).

— Who gave the beak to the bird will also provide it with food (*A Bend in the Ganges*).

Sheila said at one place in Anand's *Coolie*, 'Hot tea cools your heart in the heat of summer'—almost a literal translation of an aphorism very popular in India. To cite another example from the same book: 'You have hardly a place to rest your head on for the night and you build castles in the air like Sheikh Chilli.' These translations easily catch the reader's attention. Exaggeration is a quality shared by many of these writers and let it be noted here that exaggeration is a trait that is common to many Indians. In fact, it is because of the almost literal translations that many things that we find in these writings apparently look like trite and commonplace usages. Many of them are often indiscriminately used in our country and have hardened into cliches. Both Raja Rao and R.K. Narayan, for example, have used the expression that somebody 'is as a sister to me'. We have in Bhattachary's *So Many Hungers* ! : a golden lotus wasting in mud and filth', in Malgonkar's *A Bend in the Ganges*: 'the touch of the hand was like a flame', 'her fingers were like ice' and 'money was spent like water', and in Anand's *Coolie*: 'Why do you hide yourself like women'.

We have argued that a good translator interprets the SL and chooses the most suitable expressions. At the same time, as

Krakowian (1984) has remarked, 'some sort of modifications of a native language concept to fit a foreign language equivalent' may also be necessary. Needless to add, through translation one gets a greater awareness of the complexity of language. The right approach develops our ability to analyse the SL and we acquire a deeper insight into SL/TL transfer strategies. If these principles are not followed, what we consequently get may be rather ridiculous.

REFERENCES

Abbi, Anvita. 1977. Reduplicated Adverbs in Hindi. *Indian Linguistics*, Vol. 38, No. 3.

Arya, R.C. 1974. Conditions of Translation Equivalence. *CIEFL* Newsletter, No. 14.

Catford, J.C. 1965. *A Linguistic Theory of Translation*. London : OUP.

Chomsky, N. 1975. Knowledge of Language. In : *Language, Mind and Knowledge*. Ed. K. Ganderson. Minneapolis.

Diot, R. 1986. Humour for Intellectuals : Can it be translated? In : *WHIMSY IV: Humour Across the Disciplines*. Edit. Don. L.F. Nilsen. Arizona State Univ.

Krakowian, B. 1984. The Teacher's Mediation in Students' Vocabulary Learning. *English Teaching Forum*. 22.3.

Lehmann, W.P. 1970. Machine Translation. In : *Linguistics*. Ed. A.A. Hill. Higginbothams.

Mehrotra, R.R. 1980. Long Live Indian English ! *The Times of India,* September 21, 1980.

Mc Guire, S.B. 1980. *Translation Studies* (New Accent). Methuen.

Narita, Kyoko. 1986. English as Troublemaker for Japanese EFL, Students. In : *WHIMSY* IV. *Humour Across the Disciplines.*

Nida, E.A. 1971. Semantic Components in Translation Theory. In: *Applications of Linguistics*. Ed. E. Perren and J.L.M. Trim Cambridge

Smith, N. and Wilson, D. 1979. *Modern Linguistics*. Harmondsworth : Penguin Books.

Tosh, W. 1970. Computer Linguistics. In : *Linguistics*. Ed. A. A. Hill. Higginbothams.

Ulrych, M. 1986. Teaching Translation in the Advanced EFL Class. *English Teaching Forum*. 24.2.

Varshney, R.L. 1977. *An Introductory Textbook of Linguistics and Phonetics* : Bareilly; Students' Store.

Verma, S.K. 1978. Syntactic Irregularities in Indian English. In : *Indian Writing in English*. Ed. Ramesh Mohan, Orient Longman.

— 1980. Some observations of Englishization of Hindi. Paper presented at the second international conference on South Asian Languages and Linguistics, Hyderabad.

— 1980. Swadeshi English : Form and Function. *IL*. Vol. 41, No. 2.

Wells, H.G. 1961. *The Outline of History*. New York : Garden City Books.

12

AN ASPECT OF INDIAN ENGLISH

"By virtue of the authority 'wasted' (vested) in me ... ", said the man at the helm of an academic institution while conferring degrees upon young graduates in the convocation. Needless to say, he became the target of ridicule. The poor man was obviously not quite careful about the pronunciation of the vowel. The matter was further aggravated when he went on to say, "... I charge each and everyone of you to prove in life and in conversation worthy of the 'shame' (same)". Of course to many these mistakes will appear more coveted to make than the one committed by an official in another institution on an identical occasion when instead of B.Sc. Engineering he called out B.Sc. English. Generally, we do not mind placing accent incorrectly when speaking, as we do not realize that it exposes our speech to great perils. Let it be remembered here that accent is the distinctive character of a vowel or syllable determined by the degree or pattern of stress or musical tone. It is important to distinguish between this meaning of 'accent' and the other meaning of 'accent' in common use *e.g.*, "He speaks with a Scots accent" which means that one can notice traces of Scots dialect in his speech. It may be noted here that differences of accent are mainly differences in vowel sounds as opposed to consonants. It seems, however, that we regard this part of the job with contempt. It is true that proper placing of accent is no mean task and needs cultivation and not many of us are willing to suffer the pangs which go with it. Received pronunciation, popularly known as R.P., is generally the model in this context. Often identified with 'BBC English', R.P. is educated Southern British English and is usually equated with the correct pronunciation of the language. R.P. is considered by many also as a mark of affectation or a desire to emphasize social superiority. Undeniably, this type of pronunciation is used by only a handful of the English speaking world. It is said that a student of Professor Daniel Jones, the first President of the International Phonetic Association, visited him when Jones was on his death bed and wanted to know how many people used R.P. Daniel Jones's reply was "Two. Daniel Jones and I am looking for the second". Though made in a light vein, the remark perhaps indicates that keeping to R.P. standards is not easy. What Jones was, in fact, trying to say was that R.P. is an abstraction *i.e.*, no one person speaks exactly the same as another. The speech that Jones was most familiar with was his own, so that featured largely in his work. He would be the last person to claim that his own style of English was better than anyone else's. In a special message sent by Jones to the Institute of Research in English Teaching (in Japan) he emphasizes the fact that Public School pronunciation (*i.e.*, R.P) is not necessarily the ideal and suggests 'West of England' pronunciation or that of some recognised American standard as being more suitable. I am reminded of the advice that a priest, unduly enthusiastic about his own pronunciation, gave to his own audience while addressing the valedictory function of a school: "If you want to succeed in your life you must have a 'girl' (goal) before you": naturally an embarrassing suggestion for the young boys to follow. "Have you come here to die" (today)", said an Australian to an Indian scholar who had reached Australia that very day. The R.P. is perhaps no longer the only standard for many learners and it does not appear to be essential for the intelligibility of the English of the numerous speakers all over the world. Gimson (1978) observes : "It is time that an international form of English should be devised ... Such a model, whose origins would have no obvious national or geographical origin, would lose the disadvantage of parochiality from which, it is claimed, the British (minority) standard suffers." Widdowson (1993) feels: "... standard English is no longer the preserve of a group of people living in an offshore European island, even if some of them still deem to think that it is. It is an international language... It is a matter of considerable pride and satisfaction to the native speakers of English that their language is an international means of communication. But the point is it is only international to the extent that it is not their language. It is not a possession which they lease out to others, while still retaining the freeholds. Other people actually own it."

The boy sitting next to me wrote "My sister" when the teacher had actually said "Manchester" : this incident is associated with my first year in college as a student. A friend of mine when still a boy used to worry a great deal as he found many shops in his small town named "Hardwar" (Hardware) Stores which he later discovered, to his utter surprise, was "Hardware". Admittedly, I do not belong to the school of purists and strict disciplinarians in pronunciation aiming at absolute perfection and, at the same time, it is not necessary for us to imitate R.P. either.

Let us have, say, a different variety of English, if that cannot he helped, and I should say we have a right to it at least in respect of pronunciation because it is in this area that our English is remarkably different from British or American English. If Americans can have their own English, there is no reason why we should deprive ourselves of one. However, it is difficult to consider the term Indian English at par with the terms American English, Australian English etc. The reason is that whereas for Americans and Australians English is as much the mother-tongue as for the Britishers themselves, it is a second (or foreign) language for Indians. As for Baboo English, it is important to point out that some dictionaries say that a Baboo is an Indian clerk who writes English. We are fully entitled to an Indian brand of English—an English of our own. But language is not an end in itself and since English is the most widespread language we should aim at international intelligibility when speaking and not only all-India acceptability. International intelligibility is a proper thing to aim at as it contributes to better linguistic communication. It is said that once an Indian M.P. took his English friend to a session of Parliament. The members from various parts of India were making speeches and all the time the Englishman looked terribly bored. Then Mr. Nehru rose to speak. Suddenly, the visitor's face brightened up: "Here is somebody speaking in English", he exclaimed. The Indian M.P. was baffled. He explained to his English friend that all the members had been speaking in English. "My God", the Englishman exclaimed again, "I thought they were speaking in their own languages." An American once said, "In order to understand an Andhra man's English you have to know Telugu as well." Of course, various characteristics manifest themselves in various parts of India. Khushwant Singh had once invited a Minister in the Government of India to dine with him in a restaurant in Paris. The cafes they went to were full to overflowing. The minister noticed that many had tables laid

out on the pavements and some were unoccupied. "Shordarji", he exclaimed loudly, "if we can't shit inside let us shit outside.

To achieve greater intelligibility (internationally) we must take care of our accent, to begin with, because otherwise we are possibly not only unintelligible but also ridiculous and thereby providing others with much food for laughter. 'Standard' pronunciation of the language we speak is a great asset and an aim worth trying for. I know a bright young man who till the other day used to pronounce "Dum Dum" as 'dum dum' (tail, tail), a habit which, I should add, he has given up now. The problem is not all that simple because often we are unintelligible though quite up to the mark in speech. Such conflicting situations may be avoided by striking a note of compromise and without doing much damage to the standards. In fact, by manipulating things carefully we can find a way out though I always feel rather dubious about the possibility of manipulating any living language. However, this is what appears regarding Indian English in Monograph No. 7 of the Central Institute of English and Foreign Languages, Hyderabad, 1972, p. 10: "It must be remembered that our General Indian is not the result of accidental, undirected forces. If an organised effort is made, it might be possible to bring about certain changes or reforms in it—provided the points selected for attack are few enough and the change is sufficiently desirable." A professor once asked the booking clerk at the railway station : "Please give me a berth in the 3-tier (teea) compartment which you say 3-tier (taaer)." Many years ago an officer of the British Council declared Indian English to be "the most widespread dialect on earth" spoken not only in India but the entire South-east Asia, East Africa, the Carribbean and Fiji. A survey carried out amongst illiterate peasants and workers around Delhi revealed that, when asked what language they would like to learn, the majority opted for English.

Another officer of the British Council calls it a dangerous situation when the native speakers of English find it possible "to hear and not understand speakers of English from the Indian sub-continent". Quite few use English as a second language in India and it is expected that the next census will reveal an increase in this number. During an investigation done by an expert of Phonetics it was found that Indian English contains inaccuracies which are anything but intelligible to the native speakers. The speeches of the Indian speakers of India were recorded and the tapes were played before native speakers who wrote down what they heard. The investigation obtained some interesting results. This test also revealed that, generally speaking, we place the accent on the wrong syllable of the word *i.e.*, on the syllable which should not receive accent. Thus "Richard" was heard as "the child", "hesitate" as "had a", "develop" as "double", "decay" as "ticket", "arrive" as "arrow", "object" as "have that", "Benaras" as "When I was" and "atmosphere" as "must fear" and also as "Moscow". Some of the speakers left unstressed the words ordinarily stressed in connected speech in English and the result was disastrous because "several other" was understood as "similar" and "does unnerve" as "that I know". "Teeth" was taken as "heat", "deep" and also "deed" and "themselves" as "damsels". The horrible pronunciation of /v/ also unnerved the native speakers who tried to extract meaning out of sentences by writing "novel" as "oral", "service" as "sadness", "unnerve" as "annoy" and also "alarm", "twelve" as "dwell" and "veil" as "wheel". The writings on the buses nearer home come to mind : "Simdega bhaaya Gumla" is an obvious instance. A man once asked his neighbour, "Do you have T.B.?" ("Do you have T.V.?). Of course, "verb" is also often spoken as "bherb". As we do not aspirate /p/, /t/ and /k/ in initial stressed positions, "paint" was considered "felt", "touch" "Dutch", "Patna" "but", "card" "God", and "coat" "boot". In some cases /s/ was substituted for /z/ particularly in plurals and, as a result of which "peas" was understood as "peace", "knees" as "niece" and "keys" as "kiss." Some other misunderstandings arose out of lack of clear articulation on the part of speakers, elision of one or more syllables by them and wrong usage. Unfamiliar proper names proved to be another hindrance. To cite an example, "Krishna" was heard as "Kitchener".

In the end I must say that acquiring perfection in speech is a tedious job for everybody. I have heard of a scholarly Englishman posted to India who had mastered several Indian languages but who always pronounced the Urdu word "motafakkir" meaning "worried" as "mota faqir" which means "a fat beggar".

(*Courtesy* : AIR Ranchi)

INDEX

M

N

O

P

Q

R

S